Burt Franklin Research and Source Works Series #24

THE OFFICE OF

JUSTICE OF THE PEACE IN ENGLAND

IN ITS ORIGIN AND DEVELOPMENT

THE OFFICE OF

JUSTICE OF THE PEACE IN ENGLAND

IN ITS ORIGIN AND DEVELOPMENT

BY

CHARLES AUSTIN BEARD,

George William Curtis Fellow

Burt Franklin Research and Source Works Series #24

BURT FRANKLIN

New York 25, N. Y.

Published by
BURT FRANKLIN
514 West 113th Street
New York 25, N. Y.

o
ORIGINALLY PUBLISHED
NEW YORK - 1904

PRINTED IN THE U.S.A.

PREFACE

THE following pages constitute the partial result of a study which I began under the direction of Professor F. York Powell at Oxford University in 1898. My original purpose was to make a somewhat detailed research into English local government during the sixteenth and seventeenth centuries, and I devoted some time to an investigation of the county histories and records.

As the work progressed, I became conscious of the need of a better historical foundation, and turned my attention to a study of the justice of the peace. The undertaking was shortly afterward laid aside for three years until, as Fellow of Columbia University, I was able to continue my study, although without the aid of many sources which are available only in England. However, the limitation of the subject to the period ending with the accession of James I. has enabled me to make the work in a measure complete; for the county records now in existence, so far as I have been able to discover by personal research and correspondence, do not extend beyond the reign of Elizabeth, and the documents of that time are few and fragmentary. The chief sources like the *Statutes of the Realm, Calendars of the Rolls,* and *Rotuli Parliamentorum* have been at my disposal and I have endeavored to make use of all the important material they contain.

The method of treatment is to be explained by the fact that I have sought to trace the historical evolution of the office as well as to describe its constitution and competency.

Moreover, the point of view throughout has been that of constitutional or administrative law. For that reason no extensive account of any of the great subjects, like the poor law or the regulation of wages, has been given. Remembering the sharp admonition which M. Seignobos has given to amateurs, I have endeavored to avoid digressions and to content myself with indicating points of connection between my subject and the social and economic history of the period.

I am indebted to Professor F. York Powell and through him to the late Dr. Stubbs for valuable assistance and advice.

I have also to acknowledge the great help on historical and systematic points I have received from the lectures and suggestions of Professors Goodnow and Osgood of Columbia University. CHARLES BEARD.

Columbia University, January 10, 1904.

CONTENTS

CHAPTER I

Origin of the Office of Justice of the Peace

CHAPTER II

Establishment of the Office of Justice of the Peace

CHAPTER III

Development Until the Tudor Period

CHAPTER IV

TUDOR LEGISLATION RELATING TO THE JUSTICES

CHAPTER V

Privy Council and Justices of the Peace

PAGE

CHAPTER VI

Constitution of the Office of Justice of the Peace

CHAPTER VII

Process in the Sessions

CHAPTER VIII

Decay of Ancient Communal Institutions

CHAPTER I

Origin of the Office of Justice of the Peace

§ 1. *The King's Peace*

The office of justice of the peace was a creation of the crown.[1] It originated in the centralising and consolidating policy of the Plantagenets, and was an important factor in that long process by which all men and all institutions were brought under the direct and supreme authority of the state. Consequently, an adequate comprehension of the true position of the office in the evolution of English political society can be attained only by considering its relation to the extension of royal power and administration.

In the earliest stages of social development, the fundamental guarantee of security for person and property is the physical strength of the individual.[2] In the oldest Roman records as well as in the dooms of Athelbert of Kent and Ine of Wessex, there are unmistakable evidences of a state of society in which self-defence and self-redress of wrongs were normal.[3] The idea of a wrong being committed against the community or the state is a comparatively late

[1] Stubbs, *Constitutional History,* ii, 285; Boutmy, *English Constitution,* 113.

[2] Ihering, *Geist des römischen Rechts,* i, 109: "Der persönlichen Thatkraft gehört die Welt, in sich selbst trägt der Einzelne den Grund seines Rechts, durch sich selbst muss er es schützen, das ist die Quintessenz altrömischer Lebensanschauung."

[3] Moyle, *Imperatoris Iustiniani Institutiones,* 629; Pollock, *Oxford Lectures,* 70.

product in legal history,[1] and vestiges of archaic practices linger on for centuries after a high degree of civilisation is attained.[2] When the ties of kinship begin to bind men together in rudimentary societies, mutual responsibility for public order and for the redress of wrongs takes the place of individual responsibility.[3] After the ties of kinship are supplemented and finally superseded by territorial organisation, mutual responsibility continues as a fundamental principle of social control.[4]

The exact nature of this responsibility and the machinery by which it was secured are not clearly disclosed in the Anglo-Saxon dooms. The meaning of the several references which seem to involve responsibility is by no means certain. If there ever was a distinction between what is called *folk-peace* in continental usage and the king's peace, it is not to be discovered in the early English law books.[5] There is no way of determining whether ancient customs are being enforced or the king is devising measures of his own. The responsibilities of the kin, community, and king seem to be united early. A doom of Athelred orders the in-

[1] Pollock and Maitland, *History of English Law,* i, 46; Pollock, *Lectures,* 70.

[2] Pollock, *ibid.,* 72; Moyle, *op. cit.,* 631.

[3] Post, *Bausteine für eine allgemeine Rechtsgeschichte,* i, 160. "Die auf die Blutverwandtschaft gestützten primitiven ethnisch-morphologischen Bildungen halten sich dadurch zusammen, dass ihre Genossen sich gegenseitig Leben und Gut garantiren."

[4] Post *ibid.,* i, 160.

[5] Gneist, *Constitutional History,* 22: "In the course of the Anglo-Saxon period the king's peace took the place of the common, or people's peace (*Volksfriede*)." Pollock and Maitland, i, 46, question the evidence for such a clear-cut distinction: "We have not found English authority for any such term as folk-peace, which has sometimes been used in imitation of German writers."

habitants of a burh within which a breach of the peace occurs to pursue the malefactors and take them dead or alive; the nearest kin of the injured are bound to join the community in the pursuit; if the community fails in the execution of the law, the ealdorman is to go after the offenders; if he fails, the burden falls on the king; and if he fails the earldom is to lie in *unfrith.*[1]

With the development of the state, which is correlative with the growth of royal power and the formation of a royal administrative system, the king's peace overshadows and finally supersedes all others. The process is not so simple, however, as these large generalisations would seem to indicate, though it is true that the king's peace stood out clearly with the advance of society.[2] The feudalising forces were early at work complicating the system of police control by introducing the element of personal protection,[3] and later by carving out special jurisdictions. For example, the Palatinate of Durham was said to be in the peace of the bishop,[4] and, in mediæval usage, the manorial peace belonged to the lord or his bailiff.[5]

The king's peace was at first exceptional and extended only to certain persons, times, and places. A peculiar sanctity was early associated with the royal personage. The oldest dooms provide special penalties for offences committed

[1] Athelred, ii, 6. The translation of Liebermann, *Die Gesetze der Angelsachsen,* i, 223, is followed. It differs from that of Thorpe, *Ancient Laws and Institutes,* i, 287.

[2] Post, *op. cit.*, i, 162. "Ueberall, wo beim Zerfall der friedensgenossenschaftlichen Organisation eine königliche Gewalt kräftiger hervortritt, bildet sich ein besonderer Königsfrieden welcher zur Folge hat dass ein Friedbruch auch dem Könige gegenüber gesühnt werden muss."

[3] Jenks, *A Short History of Politics,* 54-59.

[4] Lapsley, *The County Palatine of Durham,* 32, 33.

[5] *Select Pleas in Manorial Courts,* ii, 113, 141-142, 152.

near the king or against his servants.[1] Plotting against the king's life involved forfeiture of life and goods.[2] From the royal person the peace spread outward to his house and his burh.[3] It soon came to include the churches, monasteries, great highways, and houses of important men in the kingdom. When the *fyrd* was out or the folk-moots in session, offences against public order were visited with increased penalties.[4] Widows, nuns, and clergy stood in the *grith* of the king.[5] This practice of instituting special provisions for the peace issued naturally from the royal military supremacy, but very early the king was regarded as general protector of the people by virtue of his kingship.[6]

By a gradual process, the king's peace extended until it covered the whole realm. The steps in the transition cannot be traced with certainty, but the forces at work in favor of such a development are evident enough. The church promoted the extension of royal authority partly from interest in peace and partly because of the king's favors and protection.[7] When the arm of the local court was weak and its retribution uncertain, it was a boon to the subject to be able to rely on the power in the land most effective in the enforcement of its will. Moreover, the revenue to be derived from the enlargement of his jurisdiction was certainly no small consideration in the king's mind as he brought all men and all places under his law.

[1] Athelbert, 3-7.

[2] Alfred, ii, 4; Thorpe, *Ancient Laws and Institutes,* i, 63.

[3] Alfred, ii, 7; Ine, 6; Maitland, *Domesday Book and Beyond,* 184, 193; Alfred, ii, 40.

[4] Alfred, ii, 40; Athelbert, 2; Ethelred, iii, 1; Canute, *Secular Laws,* 83.

[5] Athelbert, 1; Alfred, ii, 8; Ethelred, *passim.*

[6] Gneist, *Constitutional History,* 23, n.; Thorpe, *Laws,* ii, 305.

[7] Institutes of Polity, Thorpe, *Laws,* ii, 305.

The Norman Conquest gave England a strong ruler and many continental administrative practices.[1] William the Conqueror regarded himself as king of the nation, not the mere leader of a war band or a feudal chieftain. He decreed that peace should be observed in the land, and he made good his decree.[2] Henry I. placed the whole realm under his firm peace and ordered it observed.[3] The peace, however, was not yet of the crown; it depended upon the personality of the king. When the king died, his peace fell into abeyance until his successor secured the throne. If the king was strong, order reigned in the realm; if he was weak, discord and crime spread throughout the land.[4]

The Norman legal writers lent their support to the idea of royal peace.[5] The lawyers sought to strengthen and systematise the royal administration by eliminating irregularities and private jurisdictions,[6] and in Henry II.'s time the king's peace was so elastic that it was an easy matter to

[1] Brunner, *Entstehung der Schwurgerichte,* 396; Glasson, *La Grande Encyclopédie,* vii, 1053.

[2] *Select Charters,* 83; *Anglo-Saxon Chronicle,* anno 1087: "Amongst other things, the good order that William established is not to be forgotten; it was such that any man, who was himself aught, might travel over the kingdom with a bosomfull of gold unmolested; and no man durst kill another, however great the injury he might have received from him."

[3] *Select Charters,* 101: "Pacem firmam in toto regno meo pono et teneri amodo praecipio." By a slight error Pollock and Maitland have attributed this to Henry II., *History of English Law,* ii, 464, n.

[4] For example under Stephen, *A. S. Chronicle,* anno 1137.

[5] The author of Leges Edwardi makes the king the vicar of God and the protector of the people and the church, xvii: "Rex autem, qui vicarius Summi Regis est, ad hoc constitutus est, ut regnum et populum Domini, et super omnia, sanctam ecclesiam, regat et defendat ab injuriosis; maleficos autem destruat et evellat."

[6] Glanvill says comparatively nothing about seignorial jurisdiction. Pollock and Maitland, i, 166.

stretch it over causes which had hitherto belonged to the seignorial lords.[1]

The police power of the king did not advance alone. It was a part of that larger process by which all sorts and conditions of men and institutions were subjected to the growing dominion of the state. When Henry II. was issuing his Assizes, over-riding private jurisdictions in favor of royal officers, and struggling with the Church for supremacy, he was forging a national policy destined to secure the supremacy of the state.

However, if the crown was to be successful, the only way lay through the development of a dependent royal administration. Just as the judicial powers of the local lords could not be gathered into royal hands until competent royal judicial machinery was constructed, so the peace of the realm could become the king's only when there were enough officers throughout the land to enforce it. Naturally enough private jurisdictions were tenacious of life for more than two hundred years after Glanvill's day, but there were many forces on the side of the crown besides mere strength. By the close of the thirteenth century the increased complexity of the social organism brought additional burdens to the administrative system. The old combination of local elements: sheriffs and minor officials, courts leet, hundred and county courts, and the central elements of itinerant justices and special commissions could not cope with the new conditions arising from the natural development of the social and industrial life of the people.[2] A differentia-

[1] Pollock and Maitland, ii, 464.

[2] "Es trafen nun aber eine Reihe socialer Gründe zusammen, um das Gebiet der Polizeigewalt in dieser Periode ganz ausserordentlich zu erweitern und zu vervielfältigen." Gneist, *Geschichte und heutige Gestalt der englischen Communalverfassung,* i, 172. See also Cunningham, *Growth of English Industry and Commerce,* i, 263, 264.

tion of function was necessary for efficient administration. It became apparent that police control must be placed in the hands of officers appointed by the crown and responsible to it. For the king's peace a royal office was indispensable.

§ 2. *Conservator of the Peace.*

The beginning of this new office was made in the reign of Richard I. by Archbishop Hubert, the chief justiciar, a lawyer and statesman trained in the practical school of Henry II., and personally intimate with the great administrator.[1] Henry II. had placed the execution of his famous police measure, the Assize of Clarendon, in the hands of the sheriffs and royal justices. Following in part this Assize, Archbishop Hubert issued in 1195 a proclamation for the preservation of the peace. He sent through the realm the ancient oath requiring all men to observe the peace of the king and to assist in capturing all offenders against law and order. Knights especially assigned for the purpose were instructed to summon before themselves all

[1] He may have written the law book ascribed to Glanvill. Pollock and Maitland, i, 164. "The special importance of the ministerial career of Archbishop Hubert Walter arises from the facts, first, that being a nephew, pupil, and confidential friend of Ranulf Glanvill, the prime minister of Henry II., and having occupied a position involving constant and close intercourse with that king during the latter years of his life, he must be regarded as the person most likely to have had a thorough acquaintance with the principles that guided the reforms of Henry's reign, and as probably developing those principles in the changes or improvements which he adopted when he himself was practically supreme; and, secondly, that the period during which he either exercised the authority of the crown as justiciar, or in his offices of chancellor, archbishop, and legate, brought his powerful influence to bear on the sovereign as well as the people, was the last period of orderly government that preceded the granting of Magna Charta." Stubbs, *Hoveden*, iv, lxxvii.

men of fifteen years of age and over, and cause them to swear that they would not be outlaws, robbers, or thieves, or receivers and abettors of such, and furthermore that they would make pursuit *pro toto posse suo* whenever hue and cry was raised, and deliver all offenders to the knights assigned to receive them. The knights in turn were to surrender the prisoners into the hands of the sheriffs for safekeeping.[1] There is apparently no way of discovering whether these knights were assigned in each county, but contemporary practice justifies such a conclusion. Hoveden merely says, "*Ad haec igitur exsequenda missi sunt per singulos comitatus Angliae viri electi et fideles.*" [2] The result of this tentative experiment was successful.[3]

The theory is advanced that this assignment of knights marks the origin of the conservator of the peace,[4] and it is compatible with subsequent developments. Here is a distinct appointment of officers to take oaths for the preservation of the peace and to assist the sheriff in his police work —functions like those of the conservators before they received that fuller authority and dignity which made them justices of the peace.

This assignment of knights of the shire for local police work and the later establishment of regular conservators were not revolutionary proceedings, for during that period knights were often commissioned to deliver gaols and thus

[1] *Select Charters,* 264.

[2] Hoveden, iii. 300.

[3] *Ibid.,* iii, 300. ". . . . per sacramentum fidelium hominum de visnetis multos ceperunt, et carceribus regis incluserunt. At multi inde praemuniti et sibi male conscii fugerunt, relictis dominibus et possessionibus suis."

[4] Stubbs, i, 546. "The record thus forms an interesting link of connection between Anglo-Saxon jurisprudence and modern usage."

to do "high criminal justice."[1] In fact the age was marked by the utilisation of local institutions and persons, not as a recognition of any principles of local independence, but as a convenient and effective method of executing the central administrative policy.

The precedent set by Hubert does not seem to have been followed by the disorderly government of John, but in the reign of Henry III. the knights of the shire were used by the crown in police and administrative work. In 1227, Geoffrey de Lucy and four others were appointed justices for the examination of weirs in the Thames in Oxfordshire, Berks, Bucks, Middlesex, and Surrey, and given power to punish offenders against the provisions for the maintenance of weirs.[2] This was a work afterwards done by the justices of the peace.[3] In 1230, knights in conjunction with the sheriffs were assigned to take the assize of arms in the several counties. The commission for each county appointed from three to seven persons, and often included archbishops, bishops, abbots, and priors.[4] In 1252, by writs issued for the enforcement of watch and ward and the assize of arms it was provided that the sheriff and two knights especially assigned for the purpose should traverse the county and compel all persons above the age of fifteen to take an oath that they would arm themselves according to the amount of their lands and chattels.[5] In answering the men of Rutland, who had evidently been complaining

[1] Pollock and Maitland, i, 200.

[2] *Royal Letters of Henry III.*, i, 312.

[3] *Patent Rolls,* 15 Edw. III., 1340-43, 203. Statute 17 Ric. II., c. 9, makes the justices of the peace conservators of the statutes concerning the rivers.

[4] *Royal Letters,* i, 371-373.

[5] *Select Charters,* 371.

that wrongs of long standing had been unredressed, the king said that it was his will that quick justice should be done throughout the realm, and that the offences which had been committed in that county in his time, no matter who had committed them, should be reported to four knights whom he had assigned for the purpose of hearing them.[1] The Provisions of Oxford, established by the barons for the purpose of reforming the royal administrative system, decreed that four discreet knights should be chosen in each county to hear all complaints of wrong-doing on the part of the sheriffs and their bailiffs, and to report the results of their proceedings to the chief justiciary on his arrival in the locality.[2] Later, in 1259, when Edward and the knights sought to compel the barons composing the government to proceed with their reforms, an article to the same effect was inserted in the Provisions of Westminster,[3] but in the enrollment it was omitted.[4] This measure, however, may be classed with the many attempts to control the sheriffs rather than with the development of a centralised police system. Immediately after the treaty of peace between Henry III. and the barons in 1264, the administration passed into the hands of Simon de Montfort and writs were issued announcing the establishment of peace within the realm. With the counsel and consent of the barons it was provided that for the conservation of the peace custodians should be appointed in each county to serve until the king and barons should determine otherwise. Under this provision, the king with the counsel of the barons appointed from among those whose diligence and loyalty were known. The custodians

[1] *Royal Letters,* ii, 130.

[2] *Select Charters,* 387.

[3] *Annales Monastici,* i, *Annales Burton,* 477.

[4] Stubbs, ii, 84.

were commanded to attend carefully to everything which pertained to the conservation of the peace. They were publicly and firmly to forbid homicide, incendiarism, robbery, extortion, bearing of arms without license, and to repress all other offences against the peace under pain of disinheritance and peril of life and members. They were ordered to arrest all malefactors and keep them in safe custody awaiting orders from the crown. If necessary, the conservators could take the *posse comitatus* and even that of an adjacent county, and furthermore they were to aid the conservators of other counties on due occasion. If malefactors escaped, their names were to be sent to the crown so that the execution of justice could be carried out by central authorities.[1] When the government of Earl Simon began to break up before the increasing opposition, he sought to use the custodians to restore order. On May 28, 1265, Edward eluded his guards and in conjunction with the Mortimers, the Earl of Gloucester, and other supporters of the king, raised the standard of revolt. On June 7, writs were issued in the king's name ordering the custodians of the peace throughout the realm to take every precaution to repress the uprising.[2] Thus in police as in other matters Edward I. had experiments and precedents to profit by.[3]

As is apparent, the office of conservator of the peace had not assumed a definite and regular position in the constitution at the opening of Edward I.'s reign. The early appointment of knights for police work was but one of many tentative measures for the maintenance of local administration which finally culminated in the establishment of the

[1] Rymer, O., i, 792. *Select Charters*, 411.

[2] Rymer, O., i, 814.

[3] See also *Rot. Pat.*, Henry III., i, 326.

office of justice of the peace. The whole system of police control in this period was unorganised and not entirely separated from the idea of military service.[1] Occasionally special mandates were sent out to the inhabitants of various counties enjoining them to assist the sheriff in conserving the peace and arresting malefactors;[2] but the plan of assigning conservators was early adopted. In 1275, shortly after Edward I.'s first parliament, which enacted the important statute Westminster First, writs were sent out to each county ordering the proclamation of the statutes and provisions recently made in cities, boroughs, vills, and other suitable places, and enjoining the strict observance of them. They were to be written out and given to the bailiffs who were in turn to show them to all loyal persons in the county, and then to hand them over with the consent of the whole commonalty to the custody of two knights.[3] In 1277, when Edward was engaged in the Welsh war, writs were issued to the sheriffs of the various counties instructing them to swear to arms all the men of their respective districts with a view to the better preservation of the peace and the arrest of evil-doers. Each sheriff was ordered to have a good man elected in full county court to attend especially to the conservation of the peace. Mandates were also sent out commanding the bailiffs and men of several counties to assist the sheriffs in their police work.[4]

With that comprehensiveness which characterised the legislation of Edward I., the local police system was or-

[1] *Parliamentary Writs,* i, 193, 270, 271, 272.

[2] *Calendar of Patent Rolls,* Edward I., 1272-1281, 10, 100, 188. The local inhabitants are ordered to help the sheriff in pursuing vagabonds, murderers, and other evil-doers.

[3] *Record Reports,* 1883, 247.

[4] *Patent Rolls,* Edw. I., 1272-1281, 218.

ganised in the important statute of Winchester in 1285. The ancient communal machinery of hue and cry, watch and ward, and responsibility for military service was continued in full force. The statute provided for the assignment of justices to hear the reports of the constables on armor, suits, watches, and highways, and to present the defaults so discovered to the king to remedy.[1]

As the assignment of custodians which followed shortly after this statute involves the question of the method of appointment, the problem may be discussed at this point. The natural conclusion from the writs in general is that the *custodes* were appointed directly by the crown. Indeed, there can be no doubt of this being the method of appointment under Henry III.,[2] but in the reign of Edward I. there was an apparent break in the principle of assigned custodians of the peace. There are conclusive proofs that in a few instances at least, conservators were elected in the county court. Dr. Stubbs says, "In the fifth year of Edward I., an officer called *custos pacis* whose functions formed a stage in the growth of the office of Justice of the peace, was elected by the sheriff and community of each county in full county court,"[3] and again "the election of conservator is

[1] *Select Charters,* 470. Stubbs, ii, 123.

[2] *Select Charters,* 411. "Vos de consilio dictorum baronum nostrorum custodem nostrum assignaverimus . . . quamdiu nobis placuerit."

[3] *Constitutional History,* ii, 219, 286, citing *Rot. Pat.,* 5, Edward I., as quoted by Lambard in *Eirenarcha,* 15-17, who says "certain persons were wont to be elected conservators of the peace in full county before the sheriff, and of this kind I myself have seen certain records (in *Rot. Pat. de anno* 5, Edward I.) running in this course: First a writ to the Sheriff of Norfolk, commanding him to choose in his full county 'unum hominem de probioribus et potentioribus comitatus sui in custodem pacis.' Then another writ, directed Ballivis et fidelibus of the same county, giving unto them notice of the former writ, to the end (as it seemeth) that the bailiffs should warn the men of the county,

made in *pleno comitatu de assensu ejusdem comitatus,"* [1] quoting in support of the statement, *Tunc in pleno comitatu tuo de assensu ejusdem comitatus et de consilio Simonis de Wintonia . . . eligi facias unum alium de fidelibus regis.*[2] However, with his usual caution and accuracy he adds that "Probably the conservators were in the first instance appointed by the crown, the vacancies being filled by election." [3] The records which Dr. Stubbs makes the basis of the statement concerning the election of the conservator in open county court must be examined at length in order to be correctly understood.[4] After the enactment of the statute of Winchester in 1285, conservators were appointed to enforce it. Although no mention is made

and that they should appear at the county court to make the election. And lastly, to the conservator elected, this writ following: 'Edwardus, Dei gratia, &c., dilecto et fideli suo Johanni de Bretun, salutem: Cum vicecomes noster Norfolc. et communitas ejusdem comitatus elegerit vos in custodem pacis nostrae ibidem: vobis mandamus quod ad hoc diligenter intendatis, prout idem vicecomes vobis sciri faciet ex parte nostra, donec aliud inde praeciperimus. In cujus rei, &c.' "

[1] *Constitutional History,* ii, 239.

[2] *Parliamentary Writs,* i, 390. In the Introduction to his edition of *Hoveden,* Dr. Stubbs says: "There does not seem to be any ground for the assertion that these were at any period elective functionaries," p. ci.

[3] *Constitutional History,* ii, 286.

[4] At the request of Prof. Powell, Dr. Stubbs, in October, 1898, took the trouble to go into the whole matter again at length, and replied: "There is nothing to show that the election in the shiremoot was intended to be the normal way of appointment. And even if the election to the first vacancies was so intended, the practice of Edward I. from the 28th year and of Edward II. from the beginning of his reign must rule the interpretation of the king's right as stated by Edward II. in 1312. . . . The whole proceeding in that reign seems somewhat tentative, and there is just a chance that the king intended the statute of Winchester to be executed by elected officers, but it is only a chance." Letter dated at Cuddeston, October 28, 1898.

in the act itself of the manner of assignment, the attendant circumstances seem to indicate that they were appointed by the crown.[1] It is not probable that parliament, in devising a statute especially intended to correct abuses that had arisen from local disturbances and prejudices, would intend that the people who had been guilty of such notorious offences should elect the officers to enforce the law. While the absence of records is not evidence, it is however a significant fact that in the writs extant there are in this instance no indications of a general election by the people. The first writ issued is a commission in which the king states[2] that

[1] The Statute runs: "Forasmuch as from day to day robberies, murders, burnings and thefts be more often used than they have been heretofore, and felons cannot be attainted by the oath of jurors, which had rather suffer felonies done to strangers to pass without pain than to indite the offenders, of whom great part be people of the same country, or at least if the offenders be of another country the receivers be of places near; and they do the same because an oath is not put unto jurors, nor upon the country where such felonies were done. . . ." *Select Charters,* 473. Sometime afterward Commons, in a petition to the King, mentions the assignment of guardians of the peace "par commission nostre seignur le Roi solonc l'Estatut de Wynchestre." *Rot. Parl.*, ii, 166*a*.

[2] "Rex, dilectis et fidelibus suis Willelmo de Stirkeland et Roberto le Engleys, salutem. Cum nuper nobis apud Winton. existentibus de consilio Magnatum et Procerum regni nostri quedam statuta tunc ibidem edita ad pacis et tranquilitatis regni nostri conservacionem et ejusdem pacis perturbatorum maliciam reprimendam per totum regnum nostrum praedictum mandaverimus in singulis suis articulis custodiri firmiter et teneri, ac postmodum ex querela intellexerimus diversorum, quod statuta praedicta non sunt prout nobis et eidem regno expediret modo debito observata. Nos, nolentes quod ea que pro ejusdem regni utilitate communi provido consilio sunt provisa per subditorum negligenciam seu impericiam in perpetratorum hujusmodi continuacionem celterum remaneant non secuta, assignavimus vos ad videndum et plenius inquirendum in quibus partibus et locis in comitatu Westmoreland dicta statuta post mandatum nostrum predictum fuerint observata et in quibus non, et qui ea extunc curarunt minime observare aut observari minime permiserunt." *Parl. Writs,* i, 389, 390.

he knows from divers complaints that the statute enacted at Winchester for the conservation of the peace and the tranquility of the realm had not been strictly carried out, and assigns two knights to see to and inquire into the matter. Portions of the statute of Winchester are then recited at length. Then follows an order to the sheriff announcing to him the assignment of the conservators, and instructing him to assist the conservators in the execution of their duties.[1] After the complete assignment of the conservators appears the case of election referred to by Dr. Stubbs along with two other cases, but it will be noted that they arose under peculiar circumstances. Lawrence Basset and William de Echingham had been assigned to Sussex for the conservation of the peace, and Basset was found not to be possessed of sufficient qualifications and was consequently removed by writ. The sheriff was then ordered to have another appointed in his stead, (*poni facias.*).[2] Roger Bachworth,

[1] "Tibi praecipimus in fide qua nobis teneris firmiter injungentes quod quociens dicti fideles nostri tibi scire facient, venire facias coram eis tot et tales probos et legales homines de balliva tua per quos super articulis praedictis rei veritas melius sciri poterit et inquiri, et eis intendas et ea que ex officio suo tibi injungent sine dissimulatione quolibet exequaris. Ita quod tibi imputari non debeat aut possit quod pax nostra ibidem ob tui defectum minime observetur." These instructions are sent to the sheriff "Cum assignaverimus dilectos et fideles . . . . ad singulos articulos statutorum pro conservatione pacis regni nostri . . . . prout in litteris nostris patentibus quas eis super hoc misimus plenius continetur." *Parl. Writs,* i, 389.

[2] *Parl. Writs,* i, 390. "Rex. Vic. Sussex., salutem. Cum assignaverimus dilectos et fideles nostros L. Basset et W. de Echingham ad inquirendum in Comitatu tuo super articulis quos pro conservacione pacis nostre provideri fecimus prout in litteris nostris patentibus eis inde directis plenius continetur, ac terre et tenementa praedicti Laurensii in Comitatu praedicto sibi non sufficiant ad commorandum ibidem ad hujusmodi officium in partibus illis exequendum ut accepimus: tibi praecipimus quod loco ipsius Laurencii unum alium legalem militem de Comitatu praedicto qui officio illi intendere melius sciat et possit

who had been assigned conservator with William de Broke in Middlesex, (*quem Rex una cum Willelmo de Brok' nuper assignavit*) was unable to serve on account of illness, and a writ was issued instructing the sheriff to have another appointed, (*poni facias*).[1] Also Thomas Peverel de Berton, *nuper electus ad conservacionem pacis* in Southampton, was found incapable of serving on account of being infirm, and a writ was issued to the sheriff ordering him to cause the election of another in his place, '*in pleno comitatu tuo de assensu ejusdem comitatus et de consilio Simonis de Wintonia quem ad officium illud exequendum una cum praefato Thoma, Rex assignavit.*'[2] Thus it is seen that a conservator was *elected* to take the place of one who had been *assigned*[3] but with the counsel and consent of his colleague. It is evident that these cases as they stand cannot be made the basis for a statement that the conservators were elected as

poni facias qui praestito sacramento coram te et praefato Will' extunc ea faciet et conservet una cum praefato Will', que eidem Will' et praefato Laur' injunximus per litteras nostras praedictas."

1 "Eodem modo mandatum est Vic. Middlesex. quod loco Rogeri de Bachworth, ... poni facias unum alium legalem militem ut supra eo quod idem Rogerus senio est confectus et corporis egritudine gravatus sicut Rex constat evidenter." *Parl. Writs,* i, 390.

2 *Parl. Writs,* i, 390. "Cum Thom. Peverel de Berton. nuper electus ad conservacionem pacis regis in Comitatu Suth. juxta formam articulorum per Regem et consilium suum, inde confectorum tanta ad praesens detineatur infirmitate quod ad officium illud excercendum non sufficit ut expediret, sicut ex parte ipsius Thom. Rex est ostensus: mandatum est Vicecomiti Comitatus praedicti quod si sibi legittime constare poterit ita esse, tunc in pleno comitatu suo de assensu ejusdem comitatus et de consilio Simonis de Winton. quem ad officium illud exequendum una cum praefato Thoma Rex assignavit, loco ipsius Thome eligi facias unum alium de fidelibus Regis infra Comitatum praedictum residentem . . . ."

3 Though the word 'electus' is used in this last writ, its only translation can be that of 'assignatus,' for de Berton was assigned by the same letters patent as the other conservators.

a rule. The one clear instance of the election of a conservator appears to be that of 1277.[1] Of course election in the county court would have been no innovation in the affairs of local government and during this period special efforts were made by the commons to secure a larger measure of local independence. The right to elect even the sheriff was granted to the commons of the shire by Edward I., but it was little exercised.[2] Many of the administrative practices of Edward I.'s government had not yet hardened into settled rules.

Under Edward II., the writs and orders concerning the custodians of the peace are exceedingly numerous and show a slight progression in the functions of the office. Indeed, by the close of the reign, the business of the conservator was taking the form which it was to assume in the hands of the justice of the peace under Edward III. The commission of 1307 assigned conservators to reside in the county and visit all parts when necessary for the conservation of the peace. The statute of Winchester in all its articles, and all matters in writs and mandates grounded upon it and issued by Edward I. were to be enforced. If any disturbance arose in the county they could raise the *posse comitatus* and put the offenders into custody to await the orders of the king. Proclamation was to be made for the maintenance of the equal weight and standard of the coin of Edward I. Merchandise was not to be bought or sold at a higher rate than in the time of Edward I., because the money was as good as it was in those days. For the better enforcement of the proclamation in cities, boroughs, and market towns the conservators were given full powers

[1] *Patent Rolls,* Edward I., 1272-1281, 218, 219; see above p. 23.

[2] *Statutes of the Realm,* i, 140. Repealed in the 9th year of Edward II. Stubbs, ii, 217.

to assign from every city two citizens, from every borough two burgesses, and from every market town two good and lawful men, who after having taken the oath were strictly to enforce the commission in their respective places. Forestallers, monopolisers, and all offenders against the ordinance were to be imprisoned until orders from the king were received.[1] From year to year the powers and the functions of the conservators widened. The commission of 1308 appointed the conservators *durante bene placito.* It embodied the provisions of the statute of Winchester and the proclamation concerning the currency just as the previous commission. Offenders were to be taken into custody, and if necessary pursued by the conservators and the *posse comitatus* from hundred to hundred and from shire to shire. All bailiffs and constables in townships and hundreds were enjoined to use their best endeavor for the conservation of the peace under penalties of fine and imprisonment. Proclamation was to be made that no *proceres* or *magnates* or others, regardless of rank or condition, should take any prises of corn, oxen, sheep, or other victuals, or of horses, wagons, or other vehicles against the will of the owners. Exceptions were made to special officers of the crown, but all others who took any such prises were to have the hue and cry raised against them, as disturbers of the peace and were to be arrested and committed to the nearest gaol to await the due process of law.[2] In the commission of 1313 the conservators were especially ordered to enquire by the oaths of good and lawful men concerning disturbances and other outrages against the peace, within franchises and without, and all persons against whom indictments were found, or who were suspected notoriously

[1] *Parl. Writs,* vol. II, div. ii, part 2, pages 8 and 9.

[2] *Part. Writs,* II, ii, 2, p. 11.

were to be kept in custody by the sheriff. The conservators were required to make monthly returns to the council at Westminster of their proceedings and the names of malefactors.[1] Toward the close of the reign of Edward II., the conservators were urged to proceed with greater activity in dispersing seditious assemblies and arresting malefactors, and, in order to make the ordinance more effective, they were given power to fine and punish in any other manner, according to their discretion, all those who were disobedient or contrary.[2] Estreats of the fines were to be sent to the exchequer. Along with the commissions, writs generally went to the sheriffs instructing them to attend to and obey the commands of the conservators whenever they should be required in the king's name. They were to summon juries before the conservators at such times and places as they should require, and they were not to let prisoners out on bail except on special order from the king.[3]

In addition to the regular commissions of the peace issued to all the counties, writs were frequently sent out for the execution of special orders. In 1307, conservators were appointed in the northern counties to "resist the malice and insolence of Robert de Brus and his accomplices."[4] Special justices were sometimes appointed to hear the cases of indictments by the conservators. In some of the hundreds special conservators were appointed and empowered to pay their own charges and those of their assistants by levies upon

[1] *Parl. Writs,* II, ii, 2, pp. 74, 75.

[2] *Ibid.,* 282. "Ut autem praemissa efficacius facere valeatis, damus vobis potestatem omnes illos qui vobis inobedientes aut contrarios inveneritis in hac parte per gravia amerciamenta aut alio modo juxta discrecionem vostram castigandi et puniendi."

[3] *Parl. Writs,* II, div. ii, pt. 2, pp. 71, 76.

[4] *Ibid.,* II, i, 2, p. 369.

the inhabitants holding lands or tenements.[1] *Sub-custodes* were sometimes assigned.[2]

While under Edward II. the exact manner of appointment is not definitely stated, the circumstances seem to indicate that the right belonged to and was exercised by the crown. There are certainly no direct evidences pointing to the election of the officer, while the circumstantial evidences seem in favor of the assignment by the crown. In all the documents published in the *Parliamentary Writs* and *Close* and *Patent Rolls* there is not one (so far as I know) which orders an election during the reign of Edward II. The first document encountered in the constitution of a complete set of conservators or an individual conservator is the *assignaverimus* and that is generally followed by an announcement of the fact to the sheriff and instructions to him to assist in the maintenance of the peace. On the other hand, however, this absence of records does not prove the case. But in 1312, the king most assuredly did assert his right to appoint the conservators. A writ signed *Per ipsum Regem* was issued to all the sheriffs instructing them to inquire concerning those who asserted themselves to be keepers of the king's peace, and had not been appointed by the king, to whom the assignment of the custodians of the peace belonged. The sheriffs were ordered also to proclaim that all persons should obey the conservators chosen by the king.[3] According to the commission of 1308, the conserva-

[1] *Parl. Writs,* II, ii, pt. 2, 170.

[2] *Ibid.,* II, ii, 2, 238. Prynne, *Institutes,* gives about one hundred references to the Close and Patent Rolls concerning the conservators before Edward III. See also *Parl. Writs,* II, ii, pt. 2, pp. 28, 32, 58, 62, 71, 72, 73, 75, 76, 85, 102, 103, 148, 150, 151, 170, 238, 274, *et passim.*

[3] Rymer, ii, pt. 1, 161. Record Edition. *Parl. Writs,* II, ii, 49. "Rex vic . . . . salutem. Quia datum est nobis intelligi, quod quidam de balliva tua, custodes pacis nostri in eadem balliva asserunt se esse, ab

tors were assigned *durante bene placito.*[1] In 1320, the men of Bucks asked for the assignment of two specified persons as *custodes pacis* in that county in the place of a guardian who was not able and did not wish to serve.[2] Response was made that the chancellor and treasurer would do what appeared best in the matter. In the same year, the commonalty of Norfolk requested the removal of a conservator recently assigned, *pro eo quod se non bene gerit in officio predicto.*[3] The king responded that the negligent officer would be ousted and another assigned. While the customary practice would have required the consent of the king to the removal of a conservator elected in the county court, it is hardly probable that the commonalty, had they elected in the first place, would have chosen a person unable and unwilling to act. It is to be noticed that one of the petitions takes on the form of a recommendation of two persons, perhaps chosen by the shire. The chancellor and treasurer are not bound to accept them, however, and are left to their discretion in the matter. These various records certainly indicate that the balance of power was clearly in the hands of the crown.

aliis quam a nobis deputatos et pro talibus se gerunt, unde quam plurimum admiramur nec inmerito et movemur; cum assignatio hujusmodi custodum ad nos, et non ad alium in regno nostro pertineat facienda. Tibi precipimus, firmiter injungentes, quod secreciori et subtiliori modo quo poteris, inquiras qui sunt illi, qui pretextu alicujus commissionis alterius quam nostre se custodes pacis nostre gerunt; et de nominibus illorum, ac forma commissionis eis inde facte, nobis sub sigilo tuo distincte et aperte constare facias indilate: Facias etiam . . . publice proclamari . . . quod omnes de balliva tua custodibus pacis nostre a nobis deputatis et deputandis, et non aliis, pareant et intendant."

1 *Parl. Writs,* II, ii, pt. 2, p. 11.

2 *Rot. Parl.,* i, 373*a*.

3 *Rot. Parl.,* i, 379*a*.

CHAPTER II

Establishment of the Office of Justice of the Peace

Under the pressure of social conditions, the office of conservator of the peace was transformed into that of justice of the peace during the long reign of Edward III. A large portion of the activities of Edward's government was devoted to the maintenance of police control. It had to contend with a number of unusual disturbing forces in addition to the ordinary lawlessness which characterized the transition period. The war with France favored violence and disorder at home. Edward's method of raising troops promoted the development of livery and maintenance. He contracted with great lords to furnish large levies of soldiers for the various campaigns, and when these lords and their retainers were not on the Continent, they were continually involved in local quarrels that bordered on civil war, to say nothing of their rioting, robbing, and murdering. Had they desired to do so, the lords were scarcely able to control their followers, and generally they appeared as defenders of their retainers' quarrels and misdeeds, to the intimidation of the royal police officers and the perversion of justice. Statute after statute tells of the enormous abuses arising from this source and of earnest but futile attempts at repression.[1] Moreover, the occasional lulls in the Continental conflict permitted the return of a large number of soldiers and adventurers, flushed with victory and laden with spoils, accustomed to scenes of bloodshed and riot, and totally ur-

[1] 1 Edw. III., s. 2, c. 14; 20 Edw. III., cc. 4, 5, 6.

fitted for orderly social life. Another special disturbing factor was the Black Death which swept over England in 1348 leaving confusion and desolation in its track. With their usual exaggeration, the mediæval writers give appalling accounts of the destruction which the plague wrought. Probably from one-third to one-half of the population was actually swept away; at least, it is safe to say that the number of dead was great enough to spread disorder throughout the entire social organism. Local control was weakened by the disintegration of the manorial system, and the central government undertook the regulation of economic matters by proclamations and statutes.

The burdens of the administration were thus materially increased, but the government resolutely grappled with the problems which arose. Crown and parliament were kept busy devising methods and statutes for restraining social disorder. Almost every year a large number of special and general writs was issued to local officials and private persons giving them various duties connected with local police control.[1] The question of how best to preserve the peace of the realm was often given as one of the chief causes for summoning parliament. It appears prominently in the records of nearly every session.[2] Notwithstanding the best

[1] The *Calendars of the Patent Rolls* from 1327 to 1345 contain no less than 100 notices of documents issued by the king and council referring to maintenance of the peace.

[2] The *Roll* for 6 Edward III. is almost entirely taken up with police measures. 13 Edward III. was summoned for three main causes, dount la primere fu, Qe chescun graunt et petit endroit foi penseroit la manere coment la Pees dienz le Roialme purroit mieutz et se deveroit plus seurement, estre gardee. *Rot. Parl.*, ii, 103*a*. See also *ibid.*, ii, 64*b*, 103*a*, 158*a*, 200*a*, 225*b*, 237*a*, 268*a*. 22 Edward III., "L'autre cause est de la Pees d'Engleterre, coment et en quele manere ele se purra mieltz garder. Et sur ce fu commandez as Chivalers des Countees et autres des Communes, q'ils se deveroient treer ensemble et prendre bon avis. ii, 200*a*.

efforts of the government, complaints were constantly coming in that the commissioners of the peace were unable to cope with the wide-spread and persistent social anarchy. The total incapacity of the ancient local system and the necessity for a regular and permanent centralised administration were demonstrated beyond all question. The only solution which the government could devise was the extension of the powers of the guardians of the peace, and thus under the stress of social need, the office was advanced by stages to the position of a court of record with far-reaching powers for summary and effective action. It was quite natural also that the knights of the shire, who had assumed such a prominent part in the parliamentary government of the period, should secure to themselves the powers of local government.

The circumstances attending the dethronement of Edward II. and the coronation of his fourteen year old son led to a fear of general disorder, and the first parliament of the new reign made special provision for the conservation of the peace by passing the following act:

For the better keeping and maintenance of the peace, the king will, that in every county good men and lawful, which be [no maintainers of evil, or barretors] in the country, shall be assigned to keep the peace.[1]

In accordance with the statute, the king and council commissioned two or three in each county as guardians of the peace.[2] In Suffolk and Oxfordshire special functionaries were appointed to supervise the proceedings of these police commissioners.[3] The second parliament enacted that the

[1] 1 Edw. III., s. 2, c. 16; *Rot. Parl.*, ii, 11*a*.

[2] *Pat. Rolls*, 1327-1330, 88-90.

[3] *Ibid.*, 90. Commission to Thomas, Earl of Norfolk, marshal of England, and Edmund, Earl of Kent, the king's uncle, to supervise the proceedings of the commissioners of the peace for the county of Suffolk.

statute of Winchester and the ordinances made for the preservation of the peace were to be observed in every point; the justices assigned were to be empowered to enquire into defaults and to report them to the king and parliament; they were also given authority to punish those who resisted or disobeyed their orders.[1] Shortly afterward, full commissions were made for all the counties.[2] In the fourth year of Edward's reign parliament passed a measure providing that

> There shall be assigned good and lawful men in every county to keep the peace; and [at the time of the assignments] mention shall be made that such as shall be indicted or taken by the said keepers of the peace, shall not be let to mainprise by the sheriffs, nor by none other ministers, if they be not mainpernable by the law . . . . . And the justices assigned to deliver the gaols shall have power to deliver the same gaols of those that shall be indicted before the keepers of the peace; and that the said keepers shall send their indictments before the justices. . . . . [3]

Sometimes commissions of oyer and terminer were issued to keepers of the peace, thus giving them full power in matters pertaining to police. This practice, however, was not a general one,[4] although there was a growing consciousness of the fact that the limited authority of the conservators was not sufficient to enable them to deal with offences against the peace which required speedy and certain punishment.

So urgent were the demands for the maintenance of the

[1] 2 Edw. III., c. 6. In 1328 a number of commissions were issued and some old ones reinforced. *Pat. Rolls,* 1327-1330, 352, 355, 356.

[2] *Ibid.,* 429, May 18, 1329.

[3] 4 Edward III., c. 2. Full commission to all counties by the Council, 1331 and 1332. *Pat. Rolls,* 1330-1334, 136, 285.

[4] *Pat. Rolls,* 1330-1334, 63.

peace in the realm that the parliament, summoned in the sixth year of Edward's reign for the purpose of deliberating upon a crusade to the Holy Land, unanimously postponed the question in order to consider more pressing matters concerning the state of the kingdom. At the opening, the chancellor, Bishop of Winchester, declared the cause of the summons to be the desire of the king for the advice of the parliament on the question of the crusade. However, at the command of the king, Sir Geoffrey Scrope called the attention of parliament to the fact that it was notorious that, in defiance of the law, great companies had been organised and had wrought enormous evils on the king's subjects, the church, and his justices; that these offenders had imprisoned people to secure ransoms, had robbed and murdered others, and committed other mischiefs and felonies *en despit du Roi et en affrai de sa pees et destructioun de son people.* Scrope then charged parliament to counsel among themselves *comment sa pees poet mielz estre garde et les ditz malveis issint levez, chastiez, et refreintz de lur malice.* The clergy withdrew on the ground that matters concerning police did not belong to them. The lords and commons deliberated apart. The advice of the lords was that the king should assign lords (*grantz*) as special guardians in every county of the realm and that the sheriffs, ordinary conservators, and people should be required to aid them in their work. The special guardians were to make an array of four men and the reeve of each vill, and to enquire whether they knew of marauding companies or other offenders. The villagers on due occasion were to raise hue and cry and pursue law-breakers from vill to vill, hundred to hundred, county to county, and to arrest and detain them. If they failed in their quest, they were to inform the guardians who were then to raise the whole power of the county for the pursuit until successful. The guardians were also to be authorized to hear and determine in all cases arising before them and to punish all who disobeyed their orders or favored offenders. As an additional security the king was to ride through the land from county to county, supervise the proceedings of the guardians, and punish the culpable and disobedient. This complete and thorough-going proposal was enacted into a law. With the assent of the king and parliament, the clergy at the same time prepared and issued a sentence of excommunication against all those who disturbed the peace and quiet of the church and the realm, and especially against those who made alliances by covenant, obligations, confederations, or in any manner through malice. Those who aided in such disturbance of the peace were included.[1] Within a few days, commissions, the form of which was prepared *en pleyn Parlement*,[2] were issued appointing four or more keepers of the peace in each county, and empowering them to arrest all offenders against good order, and to hear and determine in all matters of the sort.[3] Thus many years before the statute of 34 Edward III., which is commonly regarded by commentators as the measure which originated the office of justice of the peace, county guardians had received substantially the same powers.

Notwithstanding these precautions, lawlessness continued, and the efforts of the keepers seemed futile.[4] Complaints

[1] This police measure is not included in the Record Edition of the *Statutes of the Realm*, but it was undoubtedly the law of the land. This is shown by the form which the measure took, by the fact that it received the assent of king, lords, and commons, and by the recognition of it in the commissions issued in accordance therewith. *Rot. Parl.*, ii, 65.

[2] Parry, *Parliaments and Councils*, 98.

[3] *Pat. Rolls*, 1330-1334, 292-297.

[4] *Ibid.*, 348, 445.

of the misdeeds of thieves, malefactors, and maintainers continued. In the tenth year of the reign, parliament again provided for the assignment of good and lawful men in every county to hear and determine, within the franchises as well as without, all offences against the peace.[1] Two years later, the question of how to maintain order was again the primary cause of the calling of another parliament,[2] and commons again advised strengthening the hands of the guardians of the peace and stricter methods in letting offenders out on bail.[3] In 1343, parliament, at the request of the king for advice on the state of the realm, recommended a stringent remedy for social disorder. They requested that both houses might be allowed to choose justices to keep the peace and punish malefactors. The justices so selected were to be sworn to be faithful in their office, and to be empowered to hear and determine on felonies, trespasses, conspiracies, confederacies, *malveys,* and maintenance. Parliament prepared a long list of articles expressly setting forth the work of the justices. In addition to the above matters, they were to enquire on some points touching trade, labor, and false money.[4] This provision evidently did not please the people, for in the next parliament, commons complained that the new commission of enquiry, by reason of outrageous fines and other grievances, had worked more to the destruction of the king's subjects than to the reformation of abuses. They therefore prayed that the commission should cease and a portion of the power should be transferred to keepers of the peace.[5] The king consented and

[1] 10 Edward III., *Statutes of the Realm,* i, 277.

[2] *Rot. Parl.,* ii, 103*a*.

[3] *Ibid.,* ii, 104*b*.

[4] *Ibid.,* ii, 136*b*.

[5] *Ibid.,* ii, 148*a*.

the result was a statute to the effect "that two or three of the best of reputation in the counties shall be assigned keepers of the peace by the king's commission, and at what time need shall be, the same, with other wise and learned in the law shall be assigned by king's commission to hear and determine felonies and trespasses done against the peace in the same counties, and to inflict punishment reasonably according to law and reason and the manner of the deed." [1] In 1341, commons petitioned that guardians of the peace should be assigned in each county and be given power to hear and determine on felonies and trespasses against the peace. The king consented to the assignment of guardians, but as to oyer and terminer, he adhered to the provisions of the former statute.[2]

The long series of experiments demonstrated the relative efficiency of the local gentry as guardians of the peace. True they had not accomplished all that had been expected of them, for they worked against great odds. At all events parliament could not determine upon a better method of police control. Only by concentrating power in the hands of the strong middle class of gentry independent of the great lords, could the crown hope to crush the turbulent elements in the kingdom. These progressive measures culminated in the statute of 1360 which is commonly regarded as having finally established the office of justice of the peace as a permanent police and administrative institution. It enacted

That in every county of England shall be assigned for the keeping of the peace, one lord and with him three or four of

[1] 18 Edw. III, s. 2, c. 2. Full commissions were issued at once "by petition of Parliament." *Pat. Rolls,* 1343-1345, 393.

[2] *Rot. Parl.,* ii, 161*a*.

the most worthy in the county, with some learned in the law, and they shall have power to restrain the offenders, rioters, and all other barators, and to pursue, arrest, take, and chastise them according to their trespass or offence; and to cause them to be imprisoned and duly punished according to the law and customs of the realm, and according to that which to them shall seem best to do by their discretions and good advisement; and also to inform them, and to enquire of all those that have been pillors and robbers in the parts beyond the sea, and be now come again, and go wandering, and will not labor as they were wont in times past; and to take and arrest all those that they may find by indictment, or by suspicion, and to put them in prison; and to take of all them that be [not] of good fame where they shall be found, sufficient surety and mainprise of their good behavior towards the king and his people, and the other duly to punish; to the intent that the people be not by such rioters or rebels troubled nor endamaged, nor the peace blemished, nor merchants nor other passing by the highways of the realm disturbed, nor [put in the peril which may happen] of such offenders; and also to hear and determine at the king's suit all manner of felonies and trespasses done in the same county according to the laws and customs aforesaid; and that writs of oyer and determiner be granted according to the statutes thereof made, and that the justices which shall be thereto assigned be named by the court and not by the party. And the king will that all general inquiries before this time granted within any seignories for the mischiefs and oppressions which have been done to the people by such inquiries, shall cease utterly and be repealed: and that fines which are to be made before justices for a trespass done by any person be reasonable and just, having regard to the quantity of the trespass and the causes for which they may be made.[1]

Shortly after this act, another was passed ordering the

[1] 34 Edward III., c. 1.

justices of the peace to hold their sessions four times a year.[1]

The custom of including sheriffs, undersheriffs, and gaolers in the peace commissions seems to have led to abuses and corruption, and commons accordingly petitioned that such officers should not be made guardians of the peace.[2] This may have been an attempt, however, to secure greater independence from purely royal officers in the affairs of the counties. In the last year of Edward's reign, feudalism made a strenuous protest against the wide-spread and penetrating jurisdiction of the justice of the peace. Commons petitioned that these officers should not be allowed to enquire into any matter over which the franchises of lords and towns extended, that they should be limited to the guardianship of the peace and the enforcement of labor statutes, and that for the easement of the people they should hold their sessions four times a year.[3] This reactionary measure was rejected by the Crown on the ground that such an enactment meant the annulment of previous statutes.

The question of election again arose, and though it was clearly asserted that the right of assignment would be exercised by the King alone, the matter was not finally settled.[4] In 1347, commons petitioned that the guardians of the peace with power to hear and determine felonies and trespasses should be chosen *par Gentz des Counteez,* but no response appears upon the printed Rolls.[5] In the twenty-

[1] 36 Edward III., c. 12.

[2] *Rot. Parl.,* ii, 335*b.*

[3] *Ibid.,* ii, 366*b.*

[4] Gneist, *Constitutional History,* 302, is mistaken when he states that the struggle over election closed with this reign. In 3 Richard II. Commons again petitioned that the justices should be chosen "par les seignurs et chivalers des Counties en ce Present Parlement." *Rot. Parl.,* iii, 84*a.*

[5] *Rot. Parl.,* ii, 174*b.*

eighth year of Edward III., the commons recognized the royal right of assignment in the petition that the guardians of the peace "may be made of the most loyal and sufficient men of the counties and not in foreign places, and that no justice of the peace be assigned unless he shall be of sufficient estate and condition to answer to the king and people."[1] The answer was: "As the former petition is reasonable, the lord the king willeth that it be granted." In the thirty-seventh year of Edward III., parliament sought to secure control of the election of justices of the peace. The prayer ran: "May it please the lord the king to grant to the knights of the shires, cities, and boroughs which are come to this parliament power to choose people to be justices of labourers and artificers and keepers of the peace, and that the persons chosen may not be removed by any suggestion to put others in their places who are less sufficient." The petition was answered as follows: "Let them cause convenient persons to be named in this parliament and the king will assign whom he shall please."[2] In the fiftieth year of Edward's reign commons again petitioned "that whereas the justices of the peace are assigned by brocage of the maintainers of the country who commit great outrages by maintenance to the poor people of the country, and are common maintainers of the misdoings, the said justices of the peace be named in every county by the lords and knights of the counties in parliament, and that they shall be sworn before the council of the king in the same manner that other people are; and that they shall not be removed without assent of parliament, which will turn greatly to the profit of the king; and that convenient wages may be assigned to the said justices to keep their sessions, for without wages they have

[1] *Rot. Parl.*, ii, 257*b*.

[2] *Rot. Parl.*, ii. 277*a*.

no care to keep their sessions which is a great loss to the king." The prayer again met a prompt refusal: "They shall be named by the king and his continual council, and as to wages the king will advise." [1] The firm stand taken by the king thus reserved to the central government a strong control over local administration which prepared the way for the centralising work of the Tudors after the anarchy of the fifteenth century wore itself out. The office was thereby articulated with the national system then in course of construction, and advanced co-ordinately with social and economic legislation.[2]

[1] *Rot. Parl.*, ii, 333*a*. Enough has been said to demonstrate clearly that Edward III. did not seize upon a local institution which had been developed by the people. Lambard is the source of many errors concerning the justices of the peace, which have been repeated by Blackstone, *Commentaries*, i, 351; Coke, *Institutes*, ii, 459, 558, 559, and Reeves, *History of English Law*, ii, 412. In *Eirenarcha* he says: "At common law . . . there were sundry persons that had interest in the keeping of the peace; with some it was incident to other offices, others had it simply of itself, and were named '*Custodes pacis.*'" Lambard then divides the simple officers into those holding by prescription, tenure, and election. In commenting on the act of 1 Edward III., c. 1, he says: "The act was as much as to say that in every shire the king himself should put special eyes and watches over the common people . . . . to repress all intention of uproar and force. . . . For this cause (as I think) the election of the simple Conservators or Wardens was first taken from the people and translated to the assignment of the king." *Eirenarcha*, 12, 16, 21, 22.

[2] This development is seen in the economic rather than in the constitutional history of the period. The formulation of the outlines of a nationalist policy is clearly seen in the work of parliament under Richard II. Cunningham, *op. cit.*, i, 377. The foreign policy thus adopted reacted quite naturally upon domestic legislation on economic matters, and as the old local administrative organs were not adapted to the new requirements, the justices of the peace assumed the new police and administrative functions created by the new conditions. Gneist, *Communalverfassung*, i, 181.

CHAPTER III

Development Until the Tudor Period

The parliaments of Edward III. did their best to make the office of justice of the peace an efficient police institution, and their work was thoroughly tested during the succeeding period. Maintenance, embracery, livery, brocage, forcible entry, and riots continued as apparently irrepressible abuses with which the justices were unable to deal successfully. The revived feudalism and the dynastic quarrels which fostered it had to wear themselves out before an uniform and stable administration could be maintained and peace brought to the land. Neither under Henry IV.,[1] nor under Edward IV.,[2] was there good governance in the realm; what it must have been when the civil wars were actually on may well be imagined. The justices of the peace were doubtless swayed by the forces contending for the mastery. At least the few fragments recording the actual work of the justices during the period seem to show that such was the case.[3] Fortescue deplored the practices of the great lords who "engrossed

[1] Stubbs, iii, 277.

[2] *Ibid.*, iii, 291.

[3] The justices, doubtless, did efficient work in restraining and punishing the lower orders of society, but the real disturbing forces of the time were the upper classes. It was easy enough to punish a laborer who violated a statute, but it was another matter when it came to putting down a riotous assembly fomented by a powerful lord and his retainers. Lords who were not influential enough at the centre to secure the appointment of their supporters as justices could easily overawe magistrates who refused to give the required judgment.

and broked" local offices and filled them with their own retainers and servants.[1] This abuse called forth a protest from parliament,[2] and a plaint from a political writer.[3] If justices and sheriffs showed any independence they were intimidated by force or overridden by orders wrung from the king in favor of the predominating party.[4]

§ 1. *Organisation of the Office of Justice of the Peace.*

The history of the office of justice of the peace during this period should record the changes in its internal organisation, describe its relation to the special events and movements, and give an account of the extension of its jurisdiction, so far as the available sources will permit. At the opening of his reign, Richard II. was under the influence of advisers who favored a strong administration,[5] and the house of commons, representing the most stable elements in the nation, was particularly active in the work of governing. Full commissions of the peace were issued in regular form immediately after the accession of the king.[6] In the

[1] *Monarchy,* ch. xvii.

[2] *Rot. Parl.,* iii, 444*a*.

[3] *Political Songs,* ii, 232-236.

"Now mayntenerys be made justys,
Now brocage ys made offycerys."

[4] *Paston Letters,* i, 208, 214-215. A full account of a case of intimidation on the part of Duke Clarence is preserved in the *Rolls of Parliament,* vi, 173*ab*. Ankerrette, the wife of William Twynyho, was in the peace of God and the King at her manor of Crayford, when several notorious persons, at the command of the Duke, "withoute grounde or mater ayenst all right, trouth, and conscience," carried her off seventy miles to Warwick, and without writ or warrant took her before the justices of the peace then in Sessions. They then wrung from the justices a death sentence, on a trumped-up charge, and executed the woman. The justices and jury were indemnified on the ground that they were under fear of Duke Clarence.

[5] Stubbs, ii, 461.

[6] *Patent Rolls,* 1377-1378, p. 44.

first parliament, the Archbishop of Canterbury declared that it was the purpose of the king "to maintain the laws and peace of the kingdom and to redress all that was to the contrary." [1] The Crown granted the petition of commons that the peace of the king should be securely guarded throughout the realm and that justice and right should be done to every person according to the laws of the land.[2] In 1378, commons complained that commissions of the peace were often directed to lords of the counties who, being unable to attend to the business of the sessions, appointed insufficient persons to occupy the office in their absence, and that as a result indictments were not properly returned and the realm was in disorder. In response to the petition for redress, it was promised that the chancellor, treasurer, and others of the king's council would ordain sufficient persons in each county to be justices in such cases.[3] The provision made during the reign of Edward III. for excluding sheriffs from the office of justice of the peace was confirmed on the ground that they frequently arrested men for the mere purpose of extorting fines.[4] The formulation of a measure for the preservation of the peace was given as one of the causes for the assembly of the third parliament of the reign. The king, lords, and commons proposed to enlarge the powers of the justices of the peace by giving them authority to hear and determine on extortions, confederations, maintenance, murders, and deaths *par malice purpense* without awaiting the arrival of the justices of assize, providing, however, that in difficult cases of extortion, one of the justices of either bench should be present when judg-

[1] Cobbett, *Parliamentary History*, i, 158.

[2] *Rot. Parl.*, iii, 15*a*.

[3] *Ibid.*, iii, 44*a*.

[4] *Ibid.*, iii, 64*b*.

ment was rendered. The prelates and clergy protested against the new grant of power over extortions, declaring that it had not passed with their consent and never should so pass. The king replied that he would not heed their objections, but would deal with his justices as he was wont to do in times past and was bound to do by his coronation oath.[1] Again commons made a vain attempt to secure the election of justices of the peace in parliament. The whole institution was brought under review and a complete set of documents prepared. The commission which was drawn up was full and explicit and framed in the general form which it retained until the last century.[2] According to the writ prepared in this parliament, they were to guard the peace within the liberties and without in conformity with the statutes of Winchester, Northampton, and Westminster, and to punish offenders as provided; they were to summon and bind to keep the peace those who threatened the lives and property of others; they were to enquire by wise and lawful men of the county into highway robberies, mayhem, murders, and other felonies, trespassing, forestalling, regrating, maintenance, confederacies, extortions, disturbance of the peace, weights and measures, laborers, artificers, servants, and others offending against the labor laws; and to determine and punish according to the laws, customs, and statutes of the realm. The writ prepared for the sheriff ordered him to take the oaths of the justices of the peace to the effect that they would execute the law as empowered in the commission and do justice to rich and poor without fear or favor.[3]

[1] *Rot. Parl.*, iii, 83*b*. The power over cases of extortion was given in the writ of the next year. *Rot. Parl.*, iii, 84.

[2] Gneist, *Communalverfassung*, i, 544.

[3] *Rot. Parl.*, iii, 84.

The Peasants' Revolt was now at hand, and, while the causes and events do not properly fall within the scope of this chapter, the office of justice of the peace must be considered as a factor in the repression of the uprising. The suddenness and violence of the insurrection seem to have paralysed for the time both central and local administration. When the government recovered from its fright, it called into operation the police powers at hand, but apparently did not issue special orders to the justices until the work of pacification was well on the way to completion. In September, 1381, the king commanded the keepers of the peace in the revolting counties to send to the Chancery all documents relative to the rebels, to delay judgment until further orders, and to guard the accused in prison.[1] In December, after calling attention to the rebellions, murders, and other intolerable evils which had desolated his realm, he declared that he had resolved to take effective measures to prevent a new revolt. He named keepers of the peace anew, charged them to arrest and hold in prison all who disturbed or excited the people to rebellion, to prevent by force unlawful assemblies, and to unite at need the knights, squires, and all other inhabitants of the county to march against rebels.[2] This commission was followed soon after by another of a similar character but empowering the keepers to hear and determine.[3]

The laws of Richard II. touching the organisation of the office of justice of the peace were all made in the latter half of his reign. By the last parliament held during the tutelage of the king it was enacted

[1] *Rot. Claus.*, 5 Ric. II., m. 40; Reville, *Le Soulèvement des Travailleurs*, 289.

[2] Reville, *op. cit.*, 299.

[3] *Ibid.*, 291.

That in every commission of the justice of the peace, there shall be assigned but six justices with the justices of assizes, and that the said six justices shall keep their sessions in every quarter of the year at the least, and by three days, if need be, upon pain to be punished according to the discretion of the King's Council, at the suit of every man that will complain; and that they shall enquire diligently, amongst other things touching their offices, if the said mayors, bailiffs, stewards, constables, and gaolers have duly done execution of the said ordinances [and statutes] of servants and labourers, beggars and vagabonds, and shall punish them that be punishable by the same pain of an hundred shillings by the same pain; and they that be found in default and which be not punishable by the same pain, shall be punished by their discretion; and every of the said justices shall take for their wages four shillings the day for the time of their said sessions, and their clerk two shillings of the fines and amerciaments rising and coming of the same sessions, by the hands of the sheriffs; and that the lords of franchises shall be contributory to the said wages, after the rates of their part of fines and amerciaments aforesaid; and that no steward of any lord shall be assigned in any of the said commissions, and that no association shall be made to the justices of the peace after their first commission. And it is not the intent of this statute that the justices of one Bench or of the other, nor sergeants of the law, in case that they shall be named in the said commissions, shall be bound by the force of this statute to hold the said sessions four times in the year, as the other commissioners, which be continually dwelling in the country, but that they shall do it when best they can attend.[1]

This act was followed the next year by a statute providing

That the justices of the peace shall be made of new in all

[1] 12 Ric. II., c. 10.

the counties of England of the most sufficient knights, esquires, and gentlemen of the law of the said counties.[1]

The parliament of the following year ordered that eight justices of the peace should be assigned in each county besides the lords assigned in parliament; the estreats of the justices were to be doubled and one part delivered to the sheriffs who levied the fines and paid the wages of the justices; no duke, earl, baron, or banneret holding the office of justice of the peace was henceforth to take any wages for serving.[2] This latter provision tended to make service a matter of honor, to exclude lawyers and the smaller gentry, and to consolidate the county government in the hands of the richer landed proprietors.[3]

To expedite the execution of the law, parliament, in the seventeenth year of Richard II.'s reign, passed the following measure:

Forasmuch as thieves, notoriously defamed, and others taken with the manner, by their long abiding in prison, after that they be arrested, be delivered by charters, and favorable inquests, procured to the great hindrance of the people: it is accorded and assented, that in every commission of the peace throughout the realm, where need shall be, two men of law of the same county where such commission shall be made, shall be assigned to go and proceed to the deliverance of such thieves and felons as often as they shall think it expedient.[4]

[1] 13 Ric. II., s. 1, c. 7.

[2] 14 Ric. II., c. 11. The sheriff's accounts were under the strict supervision of the Exchequer.

[3] Gneist, *Communalverfassung,* i, 181. "Der grosse Grundbesitz fand darin Entschädigung in grösserem Massstab für die absterbenden Gutsgerichte." *Ibid.,* 182.

[4] 17 Ric. II., c. 10.

The institution of justice of the peace which had served Richard so well in the repression of the Peasants' Revolt was brought into service in the last great crisis of his reign. When Henry of Lancaster landed in England ostensibly to recover his estates and redress abuses in government, he threw the country into disorder, and the king at once sent writs to the justices of the peace throughout the realm commanding them to hold their sessions, dissolve unlawful assemblies, and maintain the peace according to the statutes.[1] The outcome of the struggle showed the futility of mere royal orders when it came to a widespread disaffection with the central government.

The instrument which Richard had attempted to use against Henry and his supporters was immediately brought into service by the new king to secure the position which he had won by the force of arms, and to crush the conspiracy formed by the opposition to restore the former ruler. The minutes of the council meeting in February, 1400, record the existence of great assemblies raised by the Earls of Kent and Salisbury. In view of this state of affairs, special commissions were issued to the justices of the peace throughout the realm ordering them to repress such confederacies with a strong hand. The justices were reenforced by the association of a number of the most sufficient men in each county.[2] Henry IV.'s first parliament complained that justices were made by brocage and were maintainers of quarrels and extortionists. In response to the prayer, the king promised to charge the chancellor to make justices only from the most sufficient men of each county.[3] Con-

[1] Rymer, O., viii, 85.

[2] *Privy Council Proceedings,* i, 109; Rymer, O., viii, 124.

[3] *Rot. Parl.,* iii, 444*a*. With justices assigned by brocage and sheriffs, who packed juries to order, the local lords could have "justice" ad-

stables of castles who held commissions of the peace were accused of abusing their office by arresting and imprisoning innocent persons for the purpose of extorting fines and ransoms.[1] Parliament sought to prevent their assignment as justices, but the king decided to remedy the evil by declaring that justices of the peace should imprison only in the common gaol saving to lords their rights.[2]

Notwithstanding the comparatively strong government which Henry IV. bequeathed to his son,[3] the first parliament under Henry V. complained of the want of governance.[4] No important measure touching the constitution of the office of justice of the peace was made during the reign. A statute, however, was enacted, providing that justices should be made "of the most sufficient persons dwelling in the same counties, by the advice of the Chancellor and of the King's Council, without taking other persons dwelling in foreign counties to execute such office, except the lords and justices of assize."[5]

During the minority of Henry VI., the appointment of justices was in the hands of the Council chosen to assist in the government of the realm.[6] This provision shows a distinct recognition of the importance of the control of the justices by the authority actually in power at the centre. Another measure aiming at a closer central control was

ministered to suit themselves. "Le Viscount . . . . retourna un panell des certains persons, dount ascuns furent famuliers et ascuns tenauntz et ascuns del fee et del vesture de adversaries le dit suppliant. . . ." *Rot. Parl.*, iv, 288.

[1] *Rot. Parl.*, iii, 540*a*.

[2] 5 Henry IV., c. 10.

[3] Stubbs, iii, 74.

[4] *Rot. Parl.*, iv, 4.

[5] 2 Henry V., s. 2, c. 1.

[6] *Rot. Parl.*, iv, 176*a*.

made in the Lords' Articles. It was ordained that the justices of the peace should be changed every year, or at least named anew, and that an inquest should be made into the conduct of the justices and fines and penalties fixed for failures to execute the law.[1] The tendency of the age to concentrate the administration wholly in the hands of the upper classes and to exclude the participation of the lower orders altogether was manifested in a statute restricting the commissions of the peace to persons possessing certain property qualifications.[2] Complaints were made against the abuses in the appointment of justices of the peace, "whereof," runs the preamble, "some be of small behaviour by whom the people will not be governed nor ruled, and some for their necessity do great extortion and oppression upon the people, whereof great inconveniences be likely to arise."[3] Henceforth justices of the peace were to be required to have lands or tenements to the annual value of £20. If an unqualified person was appointed and did not report his in-

[1] *Rot. Parl.*, v, 409*b*; *Proceedings of Privy Council,* iii, 220, Article xxvi.

[2] This statute was probably placed on the same grounds as that limiting the franchise enacted during this reign. It cut both ways. While it excluded the smaller yeomanry, it also excluded the propertyless retainers of great lords. It was in harmony with the tendency to consolidate power in the hands of the better class of country gentry, upon whom the king was to rely more and more in checking the power of the turbulent nobles and building up his own royal authority. While in a way it bore the marks of feudalism in uniting property and government, it was in a new form which secured to the crown the advantages of the former without the accompanying dangers of decentralisation. If this is the true view of the development of the period, Dr. Schmidt. (*Allgemeine Staatslehre,* ii, 515), is mistaken when he regards the establishment of the office of justice of the peace as a reaction toward feudalism.

[3] As to the same complaint under Elizabeth, see Cobbett, *Parliamentary History,* i, 944-954.

ability to serve under the statute within one month from the receipt of his commission, he was liable to expulsion from office and a fine of £20.[1] The old grievance of imprisonment for purposes of extortion was again brought up in parliament, and commons petitioned that each justice of the peace should have power to let to bail persons arrested on suspicion of felony and bind them to appear at the next sessions of the peace. An attempt was made to secure for the justices of the peace as full authority as the justices of assize possessed. The proposals, however, failed to receive royal assent.[2] In the reign of Richard III., the old petitions of commons became law, and every justice was empowered to bail out at discretion persons imprisoned on suspicion of felony and the justices in sessions were authorized to enquire into cases of felons escaping from prison.[3]

§ 2. *Decay of the Norman Police System.*

The development of the office of justice of the peace was accompanied by the decay of the old Norman police system. In that system, the sheriff, co-operating with communal institutions, occupied at the outset the most important position. He exercised military, financial, judicial, and police functions. After 1194, he was aided by coroners who kept the pleas of the crown, supervised the king's local administration, and recorded the criminal doings in their counties.[4] The office of coroner did not develop into a

[1] 18 Henry VI., c. 11. This provision did not extend to justices within corporations; and if there were not enough duly qualified persons in a county, the chancellor could use his discretion.

[2] *Rot. Parl.*, v, 332*a*, 621*a*.

[3] 1 Richard III., c. 3.

[4] Pollock and Maitland, i, 534.

judicial institution; it was limited to inquests into deaths, treasure-trove, and to minor work in assisting the sheriff. The sheriff's chief court was that of the county held monthly and composed of those freeholders bound to attend.[1] Its jurisdiction was largely civil, although it attended to some preliminary business in criminal matters.[2] Below the county court was that of the hundred, which, when it was not in the hands of some lord, was under the sheriff and his bailiff. It met every three weeks and had about the same competency as the county court. Twice a year the sheriff made his turn through the hundreds from which he was not excluded for the purpose of viewing the frank-pledge and obtaining indictments against offenders. Here and there throughout each county were carved out districts differing in size over which private persons exercised jurisdiction of a varying character. Some of them had merely civil and small police powers; others could do high criminal justice. Above all these local institutions was the king's central court in its different branches.

While the whole movement of the period under consideration was in the direction of strengthening the national system under royal authority, there were special social forces at work undermining this old local system and rendering imperative the concentration of judicial and administrative business in the hands of the justices of the peace. The new national legislation on trade, labor, and police affairs could not readily be enforced by the old cumbersome local institutions. Unless specially mentioned the statutes did not fall within the competency of private jurisdictions. Moreover daily experience demonstrated the incapacity of com-

[1] Pollock and Maitland, i, 529.

[2] *Ibid.*, i, 530.

munal institutions to deal with the problems arising from the rapid individualisation of society.[1] Magna Charta took the pleas of the Crown from the sheriffs, constables, coroners, and bailiffs,[2] and the king's justice was committed to the charge of the itinerant justices or special commissions. In Coke's day, the sheriff's turn was regarded as an antiquity,[3] but the court leet continued coordinately with the justices of the peace until the nineteenth century.[4] Its powers however never expanded and covered only minor matters of local importance.

Not only did the old system decay under the growth of the power of the justices, but control of the local officers in the exercise of their remaining authority also passed into the hands of these new functionaries. The justices of the peace in quarter sessions, could investigate and punish mayors, bailiffs, stewards, constables, and gaolers who failed in the execution of the ordinances and statutes touching servants, laborers, beggars, and vagabonds.[5] They could punish sheriffs for negligence, extortion in levying the wages of knights of the shire, and violations of the various statutes limiting their powers in office.[6] Under Edward IV., com-

[1] Gneist, *Communalverfassung,* 186. "Die tägliche Erfahrung zeigte unabänderlich, dass Gemeindeversammlungen weder *in pleno* noch in *committees* eine Polizeiverwaltung in der Weise führen können, wie sie schon am Schluss des Mittelalters durch den veränderten Charakter der Friedensbewahrung, und namentlich durch die detaillirtere Gewerbe-, Arbeits- und Sittenpolizei gestaltet war. Das Aufbieten ganzer Gemeinden oder Gemeinde-Ausschüsse zu solchen Zwecken wird immer schwerfälliger und sachwidriger."

[2] Art. 24.

[3] Gneist, *Communalverfassung,* i, 186.

[4] *Ibid.,* 543.

[5] 12 Ric. II., c. 10.

[6] 23 Henry VI., cc. 9 and 10.

plaints were made against the number of vexatious and unlawful indictments made in the sheriff's turns by persons "with no conscience, freehold, and little goods," and often by sheriffs and their menials. To correct these abuses, the sheriffs and under-officials were forbidden to proceed upon indictments and presentments made in their turns, and required to deliver them all to the justices of the peace at their next sessions under a penalty of £40 for each failure to comply with the law. Justices were authorized to proceed upon such indictments, and to deliver the enrolled estreats of the fines to the sheriffs. Sheriffs arresting persons upon indictments made in the turns without process made by the justices of the peace were liable to a fine of £100.[1]

Escheators were required to have £20 in land or rent, and were forbidden to let their office to farm or to appoint deputies without vouching for them. Unqualified persons were made liable to a fine if they undertook the office, and along with other offenders against the act could be punished by the justices of the peace in sessions.[2]

§ 3. *Extension of Jurisdiction of the Justices.*

The preceding pages have dealt almost exclusively with the origin and constitution of the office of justice of the peace. The history of the institution henceforward is the

[1] 1 Edward IV., c. 2; *Rot. Parl.*, v, 494*a*. A presentment made in a turn upon the Statute of Liveries and delivered to the justices of the peace was held void on the ground that this act of Edward IV. related only to presentments which the sheriff could take by common law. Coke's *Reports*, v, 2, p. 112. The act seems to have applied primarily to criminal offences. In 2 Edward IV., Justice Moile said that a purpresture upon the king's highway or a wall made over it was a case for determination in the turn or leet. *Year Book*, 2 Edw. IV., f. 9. See also 5 Edw. IV., f. 2, and Reeves, *History of English Law*, ed. Finlason, iii, 11.

[2] 12 Edw. IV., c. 9.

record of constantly extending jurisdiction along the lines followed by the legislature in regulating labor and industry, maintaining police control, and consolidating the national administrative system. The execution of a large portion of this legislation fell upon the justices as individuals and in their sessions.

It is obviously beyond the scope of this work to digest and explain the statutes conferring powers and obligations upon the justices of the peace, for to do this would be to write the social and economic history of the period. It will therefore be necessary to limit this section to a consideration of the important branches of their jurisdiction, while indicating the sources of fuller information.

The first group of statutes falls under the general title of trade and labor regulations. At this period in English history, the control of agriculture and industry was passing from the manor and municipality to the legislature of the nation, and quite naturally the execution of the law was transferred to royal officers.[1] The regulative acts requiring uniform enforcement throughout the kingdom formed the basis of a national economic policy which began with Edward III. and lasted for centuries. No account of British trade and industry during the fifteenth and sixteenth centuries will be complete if it fails to take into consideration the value of the office of justice of the peace as an institution for maintaining that police control without which commerce is impossible.[2]

[1] Cunningham, *op. cit.*, i, 260-263.

[2] Schanz, *Englische Handelspolitik,* i, 671. "Das Mittelalter war für England keine Zeit des Stillstandes. Die öconomischen Verhältnisse zeigen einen noch unbeholfenen Charakter, aber das Sichemporringen, das Erstarken, das Streben, den überlegenen Nationen gleichzukommen, die Wahrnehmung des englischen Interesses ist auf allen Gebieten ersichtlich. Nicht den geringsten Einfluss hatte an diesem allmäligen

The depletion of the population which resulted from the Plague of 1348 called forth a series of statutes regulating the wages of laborers and artisans, fixing the prices of necessaries of life, and attaching heavy penalties for violations.[1] Apparently these statutes were enforced by special officers, known as justices of laborers, but Reeves is inclined to think that the commissions were issued to the keepers of the peace, although they had not yet received the title of justices.[2] Lambard explicitly states that the justices of laborers were not commissioners of the peace, but special justices for the cause of laborers alone and that they were not resident in the country but sent down for the time being for that work.[3] Lambard's contention is doubtless right, for it is supported by evidences other than that afforded by the internal criticism of the statutes. When commons petitioned in Edward's reign that the guardians of the peace should be taken from the better men of the county and residents, they also asked that the justices of laborers should be selected in the same manner.[4]

In the latter part of Edward III.'s reign the matter was settled definitely by an act empowering the justices of the peace in each county to hear and determine in all cases under

Wachsthum die Ausbildung der englischen Staatsverfassung. Die starke Königsgewalt und doch wieder die frühe Beschrânkung ihrer Willkür, die glückliche und zweckmässige Schaffung staatlicher Polizei- und Gerichtsorgane, die damitzusammenhängende effective Durchführung der Friedensbewahrung mussten der industriellen und commerciellen Entwicklung in hohem Masse förderlich sein."

[1] 23 Edw. III.; 25 Edw. III., s. 2, c. 1; 31 Edw. III., s. 1, c. 6; 34 Edw. III., cc. 9, 10, 11.

[2] Reeves, *History of English Law,* ii, 330.

[3] Lambard, 562.

[4] *Rot. Parl.,* ii, 257*b*. Miss Putnam, of Columbia University, in a forthcoming study of the labor movement of the time, will doubtless be able to settle the question definitely.

the statutes made for laborers and artificers, and to award damages according to the extent of the trespass.[1]

The Peasants' Revolt was not far off. The disintegrating forces which were at work breaking up the old manorial system seemed to gather strength despite the attempts to check them. Complaints were made in 1377 that the villains and land tenants were constantly withdrawing their services and refusing to abide by the old customs of the manor under pretexts arising from "evil interpretations" of the Domesday Book. Riots and confederacies were of frequent occurrence. The lords who were particularly grieved were given special commissions under the great seal to the justices of the peace to enquire of rebels, their counsellors, and maintainers, and to punish offenders.[2]

The statutes of laborers of Edward III. were confirmed at the beginning of the reign of Richard II.,[3] and later on it was enacted that "artificers, labourers, servants, and victuallers be duly justified by the justices of the peace as well at the suit of the king as of the party." Laborers and servants were forbidden to leave their respective communities without letters patent under the king's seal, which was kept by some important man of each locality under the supervision of the justices, and a penalty was provided for those who forged letters of testimony. Artificers were ordered to work in harvest time under pain of punishment at the hands of the justices.[4] The wages of artificers and laborers were rated and proclaimed in quarter sessions according to the dearth of victuals, and the proclamations thus made had the

[1] 42 Edw. III., c. 6. The justices of laborers apparently continued, however. *Rot. Parl.*, ii, 319*b*, 340-341.

[2] 1 Richard II., c. 6; Cunningham, i, 399.

[3] 2 Richard II., s. 1, c. 8.

[4] 12 Ric. II., c. 3; 7 Hen. IV., c. 17; 2 Hen. V., s. 1, c. 4; 6 Henry VI., c. 3.

force of law.[1] This act provided for the adjustment of wages on the plan of a sliding scale adjusting wages to prices, but it is questionable whether this latter provision was actually enforced.[2] This system was, however, superseded later by an act which fixed the wages of servants, laborers, and artificers, and placed the enforcement of the law in the hands of the justices of the peace.[3] It is probable that the rates thus fixed by parliament were intended to be maximum rates; while subject to these limitations, the justices could alter wages when they deemed it expedient.[4] During the reign of Henry IV. there was such a great scarcity of laborers and other servants of husbandry that the "gentlemen and other people of the realm were greatly impoverished" and as a remedy for this grievance it was enacted that parents could not apprentice their children to any trade if they did not have twenty shillings a year in land or rent. Before apprenticing their child, the parents were compelled to have a bill under the seal of two justices testifying to the value of their estates. The justices could also punish violators of the law.[5] They could issue writs to any sheriff in the kingdom ordering the arrest of fugitive laborers; they guarded the labor statutes after they had been proclaimed by the sheriffs; and in their quarter sessions, they examined laborers and masters on oath and confession, and punished them without indictments for transgression of the labor laws.[6] Agricultural laborers intending to leave

[1] 13 Ric. II., s. 1, c. 8; *Rot. Parl.*, iii, 268*b*.

[2] *English Historical Review*, ix, 312.

[3] 23 Henry VI., c. 12.

[4] Cunningham, i, 449.

[5] 7 Henry IV., c. 17; *Rot. Parl.*, iii, 602*a*; Cunningham, i, 449. This act seems to have worked a disadvantage to the chartered towns.

[6] 2 Hen. V., s. 1, c. 4. See also 2 Hen. VI., c. 18. The instances

their masters were required to engage with new masters and give due warning to the old. Twice a year, in their sessions, the justices had to proclaim all the statutes for laborers, artificers, hostlers, victuallers, servants, and vagabonds, and to set to work all who attempted to evade the laws.[1]

The work of the justices of the peace was not limited to the regulation of wages.[2] They adjusted the profits which victuallers were to receive; they punished regrators of wool and other merchandise of the Staple; they supervised the

of fugitive villains are very numerous for years after the Black Death, and inquiry into cases of this class formed an important part of the business transacted at the Halimotes. Seebohm, *English Village Community,* 30.

[1] 23 Henry VI., c. 12.

[2] The efficacy of the statutes regulating wages has been the subject of considerable discussion. *English Historical Review,* ix, 305-314. Of course the want of records precludes a final settlement of the question. The "Boke of Justyces of paes" of 1510 orders the justices of peace in their sessions to make proclamation of the wages of masons, carpenters, and other laborers. Chief Justice Hardy (1 Henry VII) considered the enforcement of the statutes for laborers among the duties of the justices. There has been unearthed in Norfolk an assessment of wages made in 9 Henry VII. "This is a copy of a very early assessment of wages, being the earliest instance we as yet know in which the justices acted upon the powers conferred by 13 Ric. II., s. 1, c. 8, a statute which, according to 6 Henry VI., c. 3, had not been executed owing to the omission of any penalty for non-observance. The latter measure, designed to remedy this defect and passed as a temporary act, was confirmed by 8 Henry VI., c. 8. . . . In less than two years there appeared this ordinance for the regulation of wages in Norfolk. That the wages thus fixed were actually paid cannot be proved, perhaps, but the inclusion of the ordinance among the entries of payments and dues is surely not without some significance as indicating that the assessment was held binding." *English Historical Review,* xiii, 299. A search among the estreat rolls preserved at London might throw some little light on the question. There is at least one as early as Henry VII. preserved.

shipment and exportation of wool and the details of the manufacture of woolen cloth.[1] They enforced the statutes regulating the preparation of leather,[2] the manufacture of arrow heads,[3] tuns, barrels, and hogsheads,[4] wax candles and images,[5] and tiles.[6]

In the nationalising movement of the time, it became necessary to bring the gilds under the control of royal officers. Parliament complained "that masters, wardens, and people of gilds, fraternities, and other companies corporate, dwelling in divers parts of the realm, oftentimes by colour of rule and governance and other terms in general words to them granted by charters and letters patent of divers kings, made among themselves many unlawful and unreasonable ordinances, as well in prices of ware and other things for their own singular profit and to the common hurt and damage of the people." As a remedy an act was passed compelling all fraternities and incorporated companies to place their letters patent and charters on record before the justices of the peace or chief governors of the towns, and forbidding masters, wardens, and others to enforce questionable ordinances until they had been discussed and approved by the justices. The justices and chief governors were further empowered to repeal or revoke any ordinance which they considered unlawful or unreasonable.[7]

[1] 4 Edward IV., c. 1; Cunningham, i, 434-438.

[2] 2 Henry VI., c. 7.

[3] 7 Henry IV., c. 7.

[4] 2 Henry VI., cc. 14, 17.

[5] 11 Henry VI., c. 12.

[6] 17 Edward IV., c. 4.

[7] 15 Hen. VI., c. 6; *Rot. Parl.*, iv, 507. Miss Kramer, of Columbia University, in a work which she is preparing on the gilds, will doubtless have some important comments on this statute.

The royal right of purveyance was a source of continual irritation from the days of the Great Charter to the reign of Charles II., and called forth a long line of statutes, which, if the complaints are to be taken seriously, were scarcely enforced at all.[1] The execution of these statutes for the most part devolved upon the justices of the peace.

Legislation against counterfeiting extends back into Anglo-Saxon times.[2] With the increase of commerce, the importance of the monetary system of the realm grew.[3] In Edward III.'s day, counterfeiting money and the king's seals was made treason.[4] In a complaint against abuses, it was declared that gold and silver coins had lost a considerable portion of their value through clipping,[5] and under Henry V., parliament sought to make the justices of the peace and assize competent to deal with all offences,[6] but the statute gave the authority to the latter, allowing the former to enquire into cases and issue writs for the arrest of those found guilty.[7] For commercial purposes, weights and measures were almost if not quite as important as the coinage, and to secure uniformity and honesty throughout the land, numer-

[1] For example: 18 Edw. III., c. 7; 4 Edw. III., c. 3; 5 Edw. III., c. 2; 25 Edw. III., s. 5, c. 2; 36 Edw. III., cc. 2, 3, 4, 5, 6; 1 Ric. II., c. 3; 7 Ric. II., c. 8; 2 Hen. IV., c. 14; 20 Hen. VI., c. 8. See also *Rot. Parl.*, iii, 15*b*, 47*a*, 93*a*, 104*a*, 115*b*, 137*a*, *passim*. The Rolls of Parliament for the 15th century do not warrant the statement that "the subject retires into the background" after the law of 1362. "Purveyance" in Palgrave, *Dict. Pol. Econ.*

[2] Athelstan, ii, c. 14, s. 1; Athelred, iv, c. 5; Cnut, ii, c. 8; Leges Hen. Primi, c. 13, s. 3.

[3] By the time of Ric. II. money was in quite general use throughout the kingdom. Cunningham, i, 457.

[4] 25 Edw. III., s. 5, c. 2.

[5] *Rot. Parl.*, iii, 126.

[6] *Ibid.*, iv, 35, 82.

[7] 4 Henry V., cc. 6, 7.

ous acts were passed by parliament. The justices of the peace were given authority to make preliminary investigation into offences, and to hear and determine.[1]

The second group of statutes may be brought together under the caption of general police control. The sources of social disorder have already been mentioned. To check the grave abuses, parliament formulated statute after statute against the disturbers of public peace, and the duties of the justices of the peace were correspondingly enlarged. No man, great or small, except certain of the king's officers, was allowed to ride armed by day or night in markets, fairs, in the presence of the King's justices, or in any part of the realm to the disturbance of the peace, and the guardians of the peace among others were ordered to enforce the act.[2] "To refrain the malice of divers people, feitors, and wandering from place to place, running in the country more abundantly than they were wont in times past," the justices were instructed to enquire concerning such offenders and "upon them to do that the law demandeth."[3] Under Richard II., the statutes against forcible entries, riots, routs, assemblies, and disturbance of the peace were confirmed, and the justices were empowered, on complaint of the party aggrieved, to take sufficient force of the county and go to the scene of the trouble. They could compel the people of the county to assist them on pain of fine and imprisonment, and they could order the sheriff to carry out their instructions. If they found the offenders, they could im-

[1] 3 Henry VI., c. 1; 11 Hen. VI., c. 8; 25 Edw. III., s. 5, c. 9; 34 Edw. III., c. 5; 13 Ric. II., s. 1, c. 9.

[2] 2 Edw. III., s. Southampton, c. 3.

[3] 7 Ric. II., c. 5; *Rot. Parl.*, iii, 158*b*. The justices could arrest, examine, and imprison wandering vagabonds or compel them to find surety until the next sessions of gaol delivery.

prison them until they made fine and ransom.[1] This act was extended during the following reign and it was provided that in case the offenders had departed before the arrival of the justices and the *posse,* the same justices should enquire diligently within a month concerning the assembly, riot, or rout, and hear and determine according to law. In case it was impossible to ascertain the truth of the matter in the inquest, two or three of the justices, the sheriff, and the under-sheriff were required to certify before the king and his council all the circumstances of the case and thus enlist the strong arm of the central authority in the enforcement of the law. The certificate so made had the same force as a presentment of twelve men. If the justices residing nearest the scene of disturbance failed to do their duty, they were made liable to a fine of £100 each.[2] Even this apparently well organised scheme failed to bring about the desired effect, for under Henry V., complaint was made that many riots and assemblies had taken place in different parts of the realm on account of the negligence of the officers charged with executing the law. The act was further strengthened by another statute providing that, in case the officers neglected their duty, on complaint of a party aggrieved, a special commission should go out under the king's seal for the investigation of the riot or assembly and also for inquiry into the defaults of the officers. The chancellor was instructed, on hearing of a riot or unlawful assembly, to issue a special writ to the justices of the peace ordering them to put the statute into execution. The

[1] 15 Ric. II., c. 2; *Rot. Parl.*, iii, 290*a*. The large number of cases in Chancery shows the failure of local officials to execute the law. *Select Cases in Chancery,* xliv.

[2] 13 Henry IV., c. 7. This act required two or three justices to carry it into effect.

local justices, moreover, were instructed to send in such information concerning riots, so that the chancery could take action in the matter.[1]

The laws against forcible entry were extended under Henry VI. and attention was called to the fact that the former statutes did not apply to peaceable entry and forcible holding or provide punishment for those who forcibly seized lands and then escaped before the arrival of the justices of the peace, or for the sheriff who did not carry out the orders of the justices. The former statutes were confirmed and the justices of the peace given authority to enquire into all cases and to oust those who had seized lands in violation of the law, and restore the lawful owners to full possession. The jury by means of which such inquiry was to be made was to be composed of "sufficient and indifferent persons dwelling next about the lands so entered." Each juror was required to have lands or tenements to the yearly value of 40s. The justices could punish sheriffs and bailiffs for negligence in the execution of their orders.[2]

Among the principal causes of mal-administration and social disturbance was the practice of livery and maintenance which persisted with remarkable tenacity during the fifteenth century in spite of the innumerable statutes enacted against it. In a proclamation Richard II. complains "of great and outrageous oppressions and maintenances made to the damage of us and of our people, in divers parts of the same realm, by divers Maintainours, Instigators, Berretors, Procurors and Embraceours of Quarrells and Inquests in the country, whereof many are the more encouraged and bold in their maintenance and evil deeds aforesaid, because that

[1] 2 Henry V., s. 1, c. 8.

[2] 8 Henry VI., c. 9.

they be of the retinue of lords and others of our said realm with Fees, Robes, and other Liveries called Liveries of Company."[1] This proclamation limited and regulated maintenance, but conferred no authority upon the justices of the peace. Later in the same reign, yeomen and other persons of a rank inferior to that of a squire, not menials in the house of a lord, were forbidden to wear the livery of a lord under pain of punishment at the hands of the justices.[2] In the next reign the justices were given power to hear and determine,[3] but the whole legislation was doubtless almost a dead letter. An act of Edward IV.'s reign confirmed all former statutes, forbade the practice altogether, and gave the justices in sessions full authority to hear complaints and punish offenders.[4]

The justices enforced the laws providing for the watches along the sea coast; and they were conservators of the rivers with full authority to appoint under-officials and to punish offenders against the various statutes.[5]

In order to provide for a thorough execution of the act against Lollards, the justices of the peace among others were required to take an oath to the effect that they would destroy and put out "all manner of heresies and errors, commonly called Lollardries, within the places where they exercised their offices and occupations from time to time with all their power." They were given authority to enquire concerning those who held "errors or heresies, as Lollards, and which be their maintainers, receivers, favorers, and sustainers, common writers of such books as well as

[1] 13 Ric. II., st. 3.

[2] 16 Ric. II., c. 4; 1 Henry IV., c. 7; *Rot. Parl.*, iii, 307*a*, 345*b*, 478*a*.

[3] 2 Henry IV., c. 22.

[4] 8 Edward IV., c. 2.

[5] 17 Ric. II., c. 9; 5 Henry IV., c. 3.

of the sermons as of their schools, conventicles, congregations, and confederacies." If the justices found a person guilty of such offences, they were to issue a *capias* to the sheriff to arrest the accused and to deliver him to the ordinaries of the place or to the commissaries for trial.[1]

Under the head of police may be included the regulation of the doings and apparel of the people of various ranks. No artificer, laborer, or other layman who did not have lands and tenements to the value of 40s. per year, no priest or cleric who did not have £10 by the year could keep dogs or outfits for hunting on pain of one year's imprisonment on conviction before the justices.[2] The justices could punish servants and laborers for playing at tennis, foot-ball, coits, dice, and "such like importune games," [3] and they assisted in the execution of the statutes regulating the apparel of the various classes of society.[4]

Such were the organization and jurisdiction of the justices of the peace at the opening of the Tudor epoch. In this office the new monarchy found an efficient and flexible instrument for carrying on the judicial and administrative work necessitated by its consolidating and centralising policy. On the broad foundation of a local class trained in the work of governing, the Tudor monarchs reared their system of absolutism. While the French kings were gathering all powers into their own hands by the use of a special class of royal officials and the repression of national councils, the Tudors were drilling and disciplining the great middle class and employing the old institutions in the service

[1] 2 Henry V., s. 1, c. 7; *Rot. Parl.*, iv, 24*a*.

[2] 13 Ric. II., s. 1, c. 13.

[3] 12 Ric. II., c. 6.

[4] 3 Edw. IV., c. 5; 22 Edw. IV., c. 1.

of the crown.[1] In every shire they had their justices chosen from the strongest and most stable element of the gentry.[2] Appointed by the crown, forced to hold office unless excused by letters patent, serving during pleasure, and liable to heavy penalties for negligence, the justices exactly met the requirements of the central autocracy. Scattered as permanent residents through every county, they possessed that intimate knowledge of local persons and conditions which facilitates efficient administration; but subject at the same time to the ever watchful scrutiny of the centre, they never secured enough corporate independence to endanger the cohesion of the national system. No continental state possessed such a combination of local independence and central control, and one is surely warranted in saying that England's early national unity and internal administrative uniformity were in a large measure due to the institution of the justice of the peace. The balance of power under the Tudors was certainly in the hands of the monarchs; but at the same time the middle and lower middle classes were being so thoroughly "drilled and regimented" in the work of the state that in the century to come they were able to assert and maintain a local independence which came to be regarded as a traditional inheritance of the English people.[3]

[1] Brewer, *Henry VIII., passim.*

[2] Stubbs, iii, 565.

[3] "With the period of the Stuarts . . . Parliament begins to aim at restricting the supreme administrative power. In another direction it is apparent that the judicial independence which resides in the honorary officers of *self-government,* by virtue of their possessions, contains the requisite energy to resist a despotic government. Finally, it becomes gradually apparent that the cohesion which the lower strata of society have gained by the local constitution of this period, both in Church and State, has engendered a manly spirit, which is able victoriously to face the constitutional struggles that ensue against absolutism in Church and State." Gneist, *Const. Hist.,* 534.

CHAPTER IV

Tudor Legislation Relating to the Justices of the Peace

Historians have for the most part devoted their attention to the more obvious movements of the Tudor epoch and have almost overlooked the importance of the work of the justices of the peace. When some scholar takes up the constitutional history of England where Dr. Stubbs left it, and writes, with the same clearness and acumen, the history of the sixteenth century, he will certainly demonstrate that the Tudor system rested upon the social control exercised by the county magistrates. The surveillance of the central government, which extended over the entire kingdom and penetrated to the lowest ranges of society, was realised and made effective only by the work of these loyal local representatives. That the justice of the peace was indeed "the State's man-of-all-work," is revealed by the most casual glance at the Statute Rolls and the records of the Privy Council proceedings.

The legislation of the Tudor period followed along certain lines of social, economic, and religious changes. It was an age of great commercial and industrial progress, and, under the Elizabethan mercantile policy, a complete system of state control was elaborated. The unsettled condition of society in the previous period had left a large number of unemployed soldiers, vagrants, and social outcasts, which was augmented by the rapid increase of enclosures.[1] The

[1] Cunningham, i, 532.

reformation, being essentially political, took many powers and duties away from the Church and transferred them to the State, thus altering the local constitution from the parish upwards. These changes were accompanied by a series of legislative enactments regulating trade and commerce, enforcing the employment of laborers, fixing wages, revising the apprenticeship system, organising the new parochial constitution, controlling local corporations, and punishing vagabonds. The rapidly extending and penetrating powers of the government touched every side of national life, and the legislation thus brought about expanded in many directions the jurisdiction of the justices of the peace.[1]

With royal favorites and sycophants at the Council and loyal justices in the provinces, the strong, centralised government of the Tudors had complete sway over the life of the people. Rebellions and riots could be discovered and checked in their incipiency; business from the most distant counties could be brought under the notice of the Council immediately; and the statutes enforced by those whose interests were at stake.[2]

Henry VII. prepared the way for his successors by the settlement of the realm and the establishment of the monarchy. He was confronted by problems which seldom disturbed his descendants. Powerful and rebellious factions had to be crushed, and general disorders, arising largely from the practices engendered by the Wars of the Roses and livery and maintenance, had to be suppressed. The kingdom needed the concentration of power in the hands of a king strong enough to maintain a strict police control

[1] Gneist, *Communalverfassung*, i, 299.

[2] For instance, the gentry who had profited by the spoils of the Church and the enclosures would naturally be interested in the suppression of heresy and the punishment of vagabonds.

and guarantee an uninterrupted administration of the law. The landed and commercial middle classes were anxious for internal order and willing to pay almost any price for it. Henry VII. fully grasped the situation,[1] and, by his police and commercial legislation, approached the stable elements of society for the purpose of winning their support in his struggle against the enemies of social peace.[2] Compared with his predecessors, he was successful.[3]

§ 1. *Organisation and Central Control of the Office.*

To carry out this policy a stricter control of local administration was rendered imperative and a great deal of early Tudor legislation was directed to that purpose. An important act was passed with a view to redress abuses brought about by the negligence and corruption of the justices of the peace.[4] The statute recites the grievances arising from the carelessness of the justices in administering their office, and provides a proclamation to be read by them four times a year in their sessions so that the people may know what is to be expected of the authorities. The proclamation states that in consequence of the failure of the justices to enforce the statutes, "the king's coin had been counterfeited, murders, robberies, felonies had been committed and done and also unlawful retainers, idleness, unlawful plays, extortions, misdemeaning of sheriffs and escheators had grown up within the realm to the great

[1] This is clearly demonstrated by Busch, *Henry VII.*

[2] Burgess, *Political Science and Constitutional Law,* i, 93.

[3] Busch, *op, cit.* "Justitiae severissimus custos, qua una re, plebem sibi maxime devinxerat, cum illà vitam ab injuriis potentiorum ac perditiorum hominum maleficio vacuam duceret." *Polydore Vergil,* 779.

[4] 4 Henry VII., c. 12.

displeasure of God, the hurt and impoverishing of the subjects and the subversion of the policy of good government." This proclamation is such an excellent statement of the actual needs of the realm, the policy of the king, and the position of the justices in the national system that a large portion of it deserves to be quoted in the language of the Statute Roll:

And his Grace considereth that a great part of the wealth and prosperity of this his land standeth in that that his subjects may live in surety under his peace in their bodies and goods, and that the husbandry of this land may increase and be upholden, which must be had by due execution of the said laws and ordinances, chargeth and commandeth all the Justices of the Peace of this his shire to endeavor them to execute the tenour of their commission, the said Laws and Ordinances ordained for the subduing of the premises, as they will stand in the love and favour of his Grace and in avoiding of the pains that be ordained if they do the contrary: And over that he chargeth and commandeth, that every man what degree or condition that he be of, that let them in word or deed to execute their said authority in any manner, form above said that they shew it to his Grace; and that if they do it not, and it come to his knowledge by other than by them they shall not be in his favour, but taken as men out of credence, and be put out of the commissions forever. And over this he chargeth and commandeth all manner of men as well the poor as the rich which be to him all one in due ministration of Justice, that is hurted or grieved in anything that the said Justices of the peace may hear or determine or execute in any wise, that he so grieved make his complaint to the Justice of the peace that next dwelleth unto him or to any of his fellows and desire remedy; and if he then have no remedy, if it be nigh such time as the Justices of Assizes come into that shire, that then he so grieved shew his complaint to the same Justices, and if then he have no remedy, or if the complaint be made long after the coming of the Justices of Assize then he so grieved come to the King's Highness or to his Chancellor for the time being and shew his grief. And his said Highness then shall send for the said Justices to know the cause why his said subjects be not eased and his laws executed, whereupon, if he find any of them in default of executing of his laws in these premises according to this his high commandment, he shall do him so offending to be put out of the commission, and further to be punished according to his demerits.[1]

Thus the king not only sought to compel the justices to execute the laws faithfully, but also to provide a sure remedy for those aggrieved, and to secure a firm grip upon the doings of the justices by opening a way to the crown itself in case of negligence or obstinacy in the lower courts.

The central review of the acts of the county magistrates was facilitated by a law which required the clerk of the peace in each shire to send into the King's Bench a brief transcript of every indictment, attainder, conviction, and outlawry for murder, robbery, felony, or other cause made before the justices of the peace.[2] This measure was supplemented by another which provided that the Lord Chancellor should appoint the *Custos Rotulorum* of each county who in turn was to choose the clerk of the peace. The importance of this measure is apparent when it is remembered that the *Custos* was the keeper of the rolls which contained an account of the doings of the justices. By having a loyal and carefully selected *Custos,* the crown was enabled to main-

[1] Coke says that "punished according to his demerits" means "that he shall be punished in an ordinary court of justice by way of indictment upon this act for contempt." *Fourth Institute,* c. 31.

[2] 34 and 35 Henry VIII., c. 14.

tain a strict supervision of the work of the local functionaries.[1] The right of certain persons to appoint justices of the peace within their liberties and jurisdictions was abrogated, with one or two exceptions, by an act of Henry VIII. which declared that all justices of the peace must be made "by letters patent under the King's Great Seal in the name and by the authority of the King's Highness . . . in all the shires, counties, counties palatine, or any other of the king's dominions at the King's will and pleasure.[2] These measures, aimed at securing direct central control, were strengthened by the law of Henry VII. vesting special jurisdiction over certain classes of offences in a delegation of the Council known as the Star Chamber and thus giving the central government an effective instrument for restraining, coercing, and punishing justices who neglected their duties or violated the law in the exercise of their functions.[3]

An attempt was made to secure a more thorough and efficient administration on the part of the justices by specialising and localising their work. They were ordered to divide their shires into districts for the better enforcement of the laws against vagabonds, retainers, unlawful games, forestallers, and regrators. Two justices at least in every district were to hold sessions in every quarter before the general sessions and to enquire into, hear, and determine all offences. Two justices in the cities and towns, not counties of themselves, were ordered to meet the county justices at least once a year to take extraordinary precautions in the execution of the law. This local work was supervised by the justices of assize,

[1] 37 Henry VIII., c. 1. [2] 27 Henry VIII., c. 24.

[3] 3 Henry VII., c. 1. Gneist, *Communalverfassung*, i, 298. Schmidt, *Allgemeine Staatslehre*, ii. 708.

who could enquire into the administration of the justices and punish them for neglect.[1]

In Henry VIII.'s reign, justices of the peace were established in Wales. The Lord Chancellor was instructed to appoint the new justices, who were to have the same power as those in England and to exercise their office in practically the same way.[2] By a later act organising the government in Wales, eight justices were to be appointed in every county in addition to the president, council, county justices, and king's attorney and solicitor.[3] The justices were to be of "good name and fame," learned in the law, and possessed of £20 annual income. In connection with their other duties, they were to appoint two constables in each hundred to assist in the conservation of the peace.

§ 2. *Consolidation of County Administration under the Justices of the Peace.*

Mention has already been made of the decay of the old communal institutions and of the tendency to concentrate the supervision of the whole county government in the hands of the justices of the peace. In the perfection of the centralised system, the Tudors found it necessary to make some one officer responsible for the entire local administration, and the justice of the peace was naturally most available for the purpose. Consequently, during this period there was a long series of acts designed to give the justices extended authority over the sheriffs, bailiffs, jurors, and other local judicial and administrative functionaries. An important statute of Henry VII. empowered the justices to examine and punish sheriffs, under-sheriffs, and shire clerks for ex-

[1] 33 Henry VIII., c. 10. [2] 27 Henry VIII., c. 5.

[3] 34 and 35 Henry VIII., c. 36, secs. 21-25.

tortion and negligence of duty, and also to supervise the books of those officials. It appears by the preamble of this act that it was a common practice for a sheriff or his subordinates to enter any number of complaints against a person when the plaintiff had really entered only one, and thereby to secure additional costs from the defendant. This abuse was forbidden under a penalty of forty shillings. Every justice of the peace was authorised upon complaint of parties aggrieved, to examine the officials concerned, and, on finding them guilty, to fine them forty shillings for every default. However, the justices themselves did not have unlimited discretion in such matters, for they were required to certify all such examinations within three months to the exchequer. The law required the sheriffs and their subordinates to give bailiffs sufficient notice to cause defendants to appear to answer to complaints, and for default the bailiffs could be fined forty shillings by the justices. The *Custos Rotulorum* or the eldest of the *Quorum* appointed two justices at the quarter sessions to supervise the books of the sheriff and undersheriffs. They were to examine the records of those officers, indent the estreats, and retain one part so that no deceit could be practised in making up returns. As a further precaution, the collectors were sworn to collect no more money than was stipulated in the sealed records and one justice could punish a defaulter in this matter. Thus the whole fiscal business of the sheriffs was brought under the direct authority of the justices, the central government given a closer grip on local finance, and the people protected against extortion.[1]

The coroner by an act of Henry VII. was allowed a certain sum of money for each dead body viewed. It appeared

[1] 11 Henry VII., c. 15.

that he had refused to enquire into cases where persons met their death by drowning or at the hands of several men, because there was little chance of securing the fees. An act of Henry VIII. declared that the coroner had no right by common law to make any charge, and he was forbidden to take a fee when a person was drowned or slain by misadventure. For any neglect of his duty he was liable to punishment at the hands of the justice of the peace.[1] Two justices, one of the *Quorum,* could hear complaints against collectors of the general levies.[2]

To meet the old evil of incompetent and packed juries, the justices in sessions were ordered to enquire into concealments of inquests, and to punish jurors who failed to return honest verdicts.[3] They could reform all panels of jurors returned before them by striking out names or making additions, and they could compel the sheriffs and underofficials to return the required persons.[4] If any one was aggrieved by perjury in an inquest, he could make a complaint against any officials, party to the corruption and perjury, by a bill before the justices of the peace who had authority to examine into the matter. The complaint was then sent to the Chancellor, who ordered the parties involved to appear before himself, the Chief Justice of either bench, the Treasurer, and the Clerk of the Rolls who had full power to examine, determine, and punish offenders. Before the case could be appealed, however, the justices of the peace were required to bind the plaintiff for the sum of costs and damages if the final decision went against him.

[1] 1 Henry VIII., c. 7.

[2] 12 Henry VII., c. 12.

[3] 3 Henry VII., c. 1.

[4] 11 Henry VII., c. 24.

§ 3. *The Justices of the Peace as an Administrative Board.*

In the reign of Henry VIII., the justices assumed the position of a board of local control or county commission, sometimes in quarter sessions and sometimes as committees. In the capacity of commissioners, justices were charged with overseeing the construction and maintenance of highways, the building of bridges, gaols, and other county structures, and a large amount of county administrative work which is at the present time attended to by the County Councils.[1] In the discharge of these duties, the justices were necessarily brought into close connection with the development of the system of local taxation.[2]

Fortifications, Highways, and Bridges. On account of the danger from invasion from Brittany and Brest, the justices and sheriff of Cornwall were ordered to make a tour of the coast from Plymouth to Land's End, and, at their discretion, to compel certain towns, boroughs, and parishes to erect fortifications. The mayors and constables, under the control of the justices, were to employ the inhabitants upon such works. The justices throughout England were to take similar precautions.[3] Until the Tudor period, parliament paid little or no attention to the construction and maintenance of highways and bridges, important as they were for the development of commerce.[4] As in Anglo-Saxon and Norman times, the obligation rested upon the communities and was poorly discharged. Failures to keep the roads in repair and damages resulting from negligence were matters within the cognisance of the local courts.[5]

[1] Anson, *Law and Custom of the Constitution,* ii, 246.

[2] *Report on Local Taxation,* 1843, pp. 5-8.

[3] 4 Henry VIII., c. 1.

[4] Schanz, *op. cit.,* i, 566.

[5] Reeves, *Hist. English Law,* iii, 11, and *Year Books* cited there.

Gneist states that the repair of bridges was a work for the county, but there were many exceptions to this rule.[1] The old law was constantly ordering the repair of bridges, but it throws little light on the method of distributing the burden.[2] According to the *Rectitudines Singularum Personarum,* "brigbotam" was a part of the service which the thegn rendered for his lands.[3] Often monasteries and gilds devoted a portion of their time and money to the maintenance of roads, bridges, and sea walls.[4] However, like most mediæval obligations, it was in general rooted in the soil or attached to certain persons or corporations. Such at least is the view which the statute mentioned below seems to warrant. The enlargement or closure of roads was brought about by a writ *ad quod damnum* addressed to the sheriff ordering him to determine by a commission of inquiry whether the change would be to the public interest.[5] The enforcement of repair was made by complaint against the responsible community or individuals in one of the king's courts, and twice a year, in turns and leets, inquests were made into the state of the roads and bridges.[6] The first attempt to bring this piece of administrative work under the justices of the peace was in the reign of Henry VIII. Four justices, one of the *Quorum,* in the regular quarter sessions were empowered to enquire into and determine cases of broken bridges. Where the responsibility for the repairs could be definitely placed, the burden was to fall upon those directly liable, but in case it could not be determined what

[1] Gneist, *Communalverfassung,* i, 282.

[2] Ethelred, v, 26; vi, 32; Cnut, c. 10, 66; Leges Hen. Primi, x, 1; xiii, 9; lxvi, 6.

[3] Thorpe, *Laws,* i, 432.

[4] Cunningham, i, 450, 522, 530 n.

[5] Gneist, *Communalverfassung*, i, 282.

[6] Schanz, i, 565–566.

"persons, lands, tenements, or bodies politic" ought to make the reparation, the justices were to call before them the constable or two of the most honest inhabitants of every town, or parish within the shire, riding, city, or town corporate, in which the bridge in question lay, and with their consent assess taxes at their discretion upon the people for the "edifying and amendment" of the structure. The justices assigned the persons to collect the taxes so laid, and appointed surveyors to attend to the repair of bridges from time to time. They could punish these under-officials for negligence or defaults.[1] They also had general powers of supervision, and could send their writs and orders into adjoining counties when it was necessary. The actual work of attending to bridges and highways was transferred by a later statute to surveyors elected by the parishioners, who were empowered to lay a proportionate tax upon the inhabitants in the form of furnishing carts and oxen and doing manual work.[2] The permanent establishment of these new functionaries relieved the justices of a portion of the detailed administration, but they retained a supervisory control. They could enquire into cases of failure to render due service and assess fines for defaults. They enforced the laws for keeping the highways in proper repair, and the information of a single justice at sessions had the force of a presentment of twelve men.[3]

[1] 22 Henry VIII., c. 5. For form of indictment and presentment, see Appendix, Nos. XI and X.

[2] 2 and 3 Philip and Mary, c. 8; 5 Eliz., c. 13; 29 Eliz., c. 5. "Thus the same bases of a parochial constitution were laid as in the case of the poor-law system, namely, the parish as the district; the surveyors as local officers, elected by the members of the community, liable as responsible representatives of the communal duty; performance in kind in proportion to the size of the household and real estate. . . ." Gneist, *Con. Hist.*, 526.

[3] 5 Eliz., c. 13.

Gaols, Houses of Correction, and County Buildings. By an act of Henry VIII., the justices in certain counties were given authority to decide what towns should have gaols, and to call before them all the high constables, tithing men, or boroughmen of every local unit and, by their consent and agreement, determine upon the money required for the proposed gaol. They could lay the necessary tax, appoint the collectors for the levy and the surveyors for the erection of the structure, and punish all officers concerned for defaults.[1]

At the close of Elizabeth's reign, all statutes for the maintenance and erection of houses of correction were repealed and one comprehensive measure enacted. It empowered the justices in their quarter sessions to order the erection of one or more houses of correction within their respective counties or cities, to provide the necessary money and materials for the construction of the same, and to supervise the work of building. The government of the houses, the establishment of rules for the correction and punishment of offenders, and all necessary orders pertaining to the same were made in the quarter sessions.[2]

Public Houses. With Henry VII. began the long list of statutes designed to regulate public houses. The justices of the peace were empowered to punish the keepers of houses where unlawful games were played, to reject the common selling of ale in towns when they considered it convenient, and to take the surety of public-house keepers to keep the peace.[3] A license system and stricter control were provided under an act of Edward VI. Two justices in every shire, city, borough, town corporate, franchise, and liberty could remove and close up tippling houses whenever they saw fit.

[1] 23 Henry VIII., c. 2.

[2] 39 and 40 Eliz., c. 4.

[3] 11 Henry VII., c. 2; 19 Henry VII., c. 12.

No person was allowed to keep such a house without a license issued in quarter sessions or by at least two justices, and for the maintenance of good order and prevention of unlawful games, all license holders were compelled to give bond before the justices. Such bonds were drawn up in quarter sessions and remained on record there, and from time to time the justices were to enquire whether the terms had been complied with and punish those license holders who were found in default. A heavy penalty of imprisonment to be imposed by the justices was laid on all persons who opened and conducted public houses without license.[1]

§ 4. *Justices of the Peace and the Parochial System.*

In the Tudor process of organisation and consolidation which extended to the lowest ecclesiastical division, the parish was brought along with other church institutions into the constitution of the state. A complete national system from the humblest office of the parish to the Star Chamber and Privy Council was built up, and in this carefully articulated hierarchy, the justices of the peace were the important connecting link between the Crown and the community.[2] Under this strong central control local functionaries were disciplined in administration and self-government so that, in the century to come, local independence was so thoroughly established that encroachments on every side could be successfully resisted.

Control of the Poor and Vagrant Classes. With the

[1] 5 and 6 Edward VI., c. 25. For form of indictment, see Appendix, No. XIII.

[2] On this most important constitutional development, see Gneist, *Constitutional History,* chapter xxxvi, and *Communalverfassung,* i, 267-291.

break-up of the more or less rigid feudal system and the development of a landless and tool-less population, the questions of vagrancy and poor maintenance became matters of increasing importance. It was in connection with the attempts of the state to deal with the new problems that the justices of the peace entered into their closest and most marked relation with the newly developed parochial system. Legislation before the Tudor period had recognised the poor and vagrant classes only to enact stringent laws against them without making any special provision for their care which, until the breach with Rome, had been the special charge of the church.[1] Systematic legislation on the subject may be said to have begun in 1530-31.[2] The preamble of the statute passed in that year runs as follows: "Where in all places throughout this realm of England, vagabonds and beggars have of long time increased and daily do increase in great and excessive numbers by the occasion of idleness, mother and root of all vices, whereby hath insurged and sprung and daily insurgeth and springeth continual thefts, murders, and other heinous offences and great enormities to the high displeasure of God and the inquieta-

[1] 23 Edward III., c. 7; 12 Ric. II., c. 7; Stubbs, iii, 619-623. Cunningham regards the admonition of parliament to the monasteries to perform their duties better as an indication that they were negligent in the discharge of their religious obligations. *Trade and Commerce*, i, 377. To the same effect, Ashley, *Economic History*, I, ii, 310. See also *Social England*, iii, 251. It appears that in the fifteenth century the towns had made some attempts to take care of their defectives and delinquents. Not a few private benefactions for the same purpose were made. Cunningham, i, 408.

[2] The old law did not take the same attitude toward the impotent poor that it did toward the sturdy vagabond. It sought to provide some relief for the former by compelling them to go into the hundred where they were born or had lived for the previous three years. Begging elsewhere was forbidden. 19 Henry VII., c. 12.

tion and damage of the king's people and to the marvelous disturbance of the common weal of this realm . . . ." In view of this state of affairs, the justices of the peace were ordered to divide their respective shires into districts among themselves, and to enquire within their limits of all aged poor and impotent persons who lived of necessity upon charity. Such persons were to be licensed to beg within certain limits, but were forbidden to go beyond their confines on pain of being set in the stocks or whipped. Those who were "hole and mightie in body and able to labour" and yet begged and wandered about without any attempts at industry were to be whipped and sent to their birthplaces or to the towns where they last dwelt for three years. The beggar so punished was given a certificate to the effect that he had paid the lawful penalty. Scholars unauthorized to beg by a university, sailors, fortune-tellers, proctors, and pardoners going about without sufficient warrant, and all other idle wanderers were to be whipped for two days together on an order from two justices of the peace; for the second offence each vagrant was to be whipped, set in pillory and lose an ear; and for the third offence he was to receive the whip and pillory, and lose the other ear. Penalties were imposed for harboring and assisting beggars, and the enforcement of the entire act in all its clauses was placed in the hands of the justices.[1] Five years later, attention was called to the fact that this statute made no provision for the employment of the sturdy beggars and the maintenance of the impotent poor. A law was then passed requiring city and parish officials to arrange for the support of the impotent and to set the sturdy and valiant to work. Officers and church-wardens were instructed to gather voluntary alms for the poor, lame, feeble, and sick

[1] 22 Henry VIII., c. 12.

so that they would not be compelled to beg. Children from five to fourteen years of age could be let out to masters, and if they resisted or deserted they were liable to be whipped on the order of the justices. If the officer refused to inflict the punishment, he could be set in stocks for his obstinacy. The justices and other officers were to direct night searches for rufflers, vagabonds, and other suspects, and punish all such offenders. Persistent vagrants were to be proceeded against by the justices just as in cases of felony.[1] In order to give employment to the poor and to encourage the weaving industry, all persons occupying land for tillage were required to sow one quarter of an acre of flax for every sixty acres under pain of punishment at the hands of the justices.[2]

The first poor law of Edward VI. recites the inefficiency of the previous acts on account of the "foolish pytie and mercy" of those whose business it was to enforce the statutes. It went on to repeal the acts of Henry VIII. and provide stringent regulations with a long train of penalties extending from branding with a hot iron to death for felony. This law was soon repealed, however, and that of Henry VIII. revived with some additions.[3] Any person who took a child from a beggar and presented it to quarter sessions could be appointed its guardian or master at the discretion of the justices. The justices could punish the child for leaving its master or its parents for enticing it away, and they could also discharge it from the bound service on misconduct of the master. Laborers who refused to work for reasonable wages were to be punished as "strong and mightie vacabonds;" sick and aged poor were to be re-

[1] 27 Henry VIII., c. 25. [2] 24 Henry VIII., c. 4.

[3] 1 Edward VI., c. 3. It provided punishment for vagrants and relief for the poor and impotent.

lieved by the parishes where they were born; and lepers and bed-ridden poor were to be permitted to beg by proctors.[1] Two years later, alms-giving, hitherto voluntary, became practically compulsory.[2] The collectors were "to gently aske and demaund of every man or woman what they would be content to geve weekly toward the relief of the poor." Persons refusing this request were to be admonished by the vicar, and if the admonition failed to produce the desired result, the bishop of the diocese was to take the matter in hand and reform the offender.

The poor law received some attention during Mary's reign. An advance was made in the direction of a definite compulsory rate. Collectors of the rate were to be elected and refusal to serve laid them liable to a fine of forty shillings by the justices. If a parish was not rich enough to support its dependents, the justices could examine into its claim, and issue licenses to the poor allowing them to beg within certain other districts. The wealthier parishes were to be persuaded to assist those overburdened with poor.[3] A number of experiments were made during the reign of Elizabeth, and the various tentative measures finally culminated in a series of thoroughly organised and comprehensive statutes. By an act in the fifth year, the justices were empowered to tax a parishioner who refused to pay his poor rate and commit him to prison if he persisted.[4] The crowning poor law of the whole period, some of the essential principles of which prevail to-day, was 39 and 40 Elizabeth c. 3.

[1] 3 and 4 Edward VI., c. 16. [2] 5 and 6 Edward VI., c. 2.

[3] 2 and 3 P. and M., c. 5.

[4] 5 Elizabeth, c. 3; 14 Eliz., c. 5. This act required the justices to keep a register of the dependents, ascertain the weekly charge of maintenance, assess the amount upon the inhabitants, and appoint overseers.

By this act the parish was retained as the lowest unit for poor-law administration and upon it was thrown the financial burden. The local execution of the law was placed in charge of overseers of the poor nominated yearly by two justices of the peace, one of the *Quorum,* who were residents of the parish or at least nearby. The overseers so chosen were to act under the complete supervision of the justices of the peace in the performance of their duties, which may be summarised as follows: they were to put to work the children of parents too poor to support them and all other persons without means of support, and to supply a stock of materials for the employment of the poor; they could tax the inhabitants of the parish and the occupiers of lands for the support of the poor and impotent, and do "all other things . . . . . concerning the premises as to them shall seem convenient." The overseers with the permission of a lord of a manor in which there was waste land, could make provisions for the erection of poorhouses. In the execution of this act, the duties of the justices of the peace were mostly supervisory and corrective. They were to require a strict account from the overseers, and in case any parish was not able to pay the required assessment, the justices in quarter sessions could assess any other parish or number of parishes for the benefit of the poor community. They could commit to prison any person who made default in payment of the assessment, and they could punish the church wardens who did not give full reports of the finances according to the law. They were to hear all complaints against the overseers and to send to the house of correction all persons who refused to work under the orders of the overseers. In the quarter sessions, the justices could rate the parishes and force the collection of money for the poor prisoners at the King's Bench, and for the support of county hospitals and almshouses. The money so collected was to be delivered to two justices chosen as treasurers. These treasurers were to pay a portion of the money to the Lord Chief Justice, disburse the remainder according to the statute, and render an account of the business to quarter sessions. This general measure was altered in no essential principle by an act a few years later,[1] and so it may be regarded as marking the culmination of the powers of the justices of the peace as poor-law administrators under the Tudors.

Closely connected with this act was another providing for the employment of the vagrant class. From time to time laws had been made for the punishment of vagabonds and the erection of houses of correction, but all these measures were repealed under Elizabeth and a comprehensive statute supplementing the poor law substituted. The justices of the peace in quarter sessions were empowered to provide for the erection, maintenance, and government of houses of correction.[2] The act also defined who should be considered rogues, vagabonds, and sturdy beggars, and gave every justice power to apprehend any wandering idler, and to have him stripped to the waist, whipped until bloody, and then sent to the place of his birth, or to the parish through which he last passed without punishment. After administering this sharp admonition to the sturdy offender, the justice was to issue a testimonial of the fact to the beggar and also to have a record kept by the minister of the parish.[3] In case the rogue was a dangerous character, two of the justices could commit him to gaol or the house of correction

[1] 43 and 44 Eliz., c. 2. A penalty of £5 was provided for justices who failed to nominate overseers. Art. ix.

[2] 39 and 40 Eliz., c. 4.

[3] For a testimonial, see Appendix V.

to await quarter sessions. If convicted there, banishment from the realm followed.[1]

Along with the care of the ordinary poor, there was the additional burden incurred by the Spanish war and the defence of England against the Armada, which threw a large number of indigent and wounded soldiers and sailors upon the state support.[2] The preamble of the act runs, "It is agreeable with Christian charity, policy, and the honour of our nation that such as have since March 25, 1588 adventured their lives and lost their limbs or disabled their bodies, or shall hereafter adventure their lives, lose their limbs or disable their bodies in the defence and service of Her Majesty and the State should at their return be relieved and rewarded to the end that they may reap the fruit of their good deserving and others may be encouraged to perform like endeavors." Soldiers deemed worthy of support were to be selected by the justices of the peace who were empowered to lay taxes for the purpose. All funds raised for the maintenance of soldiers were charged upon the parishes and the rates so levied could be collected if necessary by distress and sale of goods. Two justices were appointed treasurers for the pension and relief fund by the justices in quarter sessions.

By this extensive poor-law legislation, the measures for highways and bridges, and the local rates entailed by these two branches of administration, the constitution and functions of the parish were determined. The whole trend of the laws was in the direction of laying the burdens upon specific communities and officers, under the direct and full control of the justices of the peace, thus giving the latter

[1] 39 and 40 Eliz., c. 4. On the efficacy of these acts, see Cunningham, ii, 60, 61.

[2] 35 Eliz., c. 4; also 39 Eliz., cc. 17, 21, and 43 Eliz., c. 3.

supervisory and corrective powers without entailing too much administrative detail upon them.

§ 5. *Justices of the Peace and Trade and Labor Regulations.*

The beginnings of the regulation of trade and industry upon mercantilist principles were made in the reign of Richard II.,[1] and throughout the fifteenth century the idea of state protection came prominently into the foreground. There is to be found in the records an increasing consciousness of nationality and a growing pride in English virtues and exploits as opposed to those of the continent. The rise of Spain and the formation of French unity added to the international rivalry, and naturally turned the attention of statesmen to a consideration of the best methods of strengthening the power of England.[2] However, under the first four Tudors, trade and labor legislation made no radical departure from that of the preceding century; it was not consistent with itself or based consciously upon a broad constructive policy. It was not until Elizabeth's reign that the tentative and incomplete measures of the later middle ages were superseded by a well articulated national system, comprehensive and flexible enough to maintain its essential identity until the industrial revolution of the nineteenth century.[3] Control of wages and prices, regulation of the processes of industry, stimulation of agriculture, encouragement of shipping, and maintenance of social peace were the great topics which received the attention of Tudor parliaments. The execution of the laws which this far-reach-

[1] Cunningham, i, 392-396.

[2] Among the papers of Thomas Cromwell were found three important tracts upon trade and industry.

[3] Cunningham, ii, 16.

ing policy created fell upon the justices of the peace in so far as they involved matters of local administration.

Wages and Prices. By the labor statute of the eleventh year of Henry VII.'s reign, the wages of laborers and artisans were regulated, and any one who refused to work at the legal scale or took or paid unlawful wages was liable to a fine of twenty shillings upon conviction before the justices of the peace in sessions.[1] The act of 1514 marked no special advance upon this law except that it empowered two justices out of sessions to investigate all cases which arose under the statute.[2] Fares on the Thames boats and the wages of watermen were under the supervision of the justices.[3] In the reign of Edward VI. a severe blow was struck at combinations of laborers. The complaint was made that artificers, handicraftsmen, and laborers had made confederacies and sworn mutual oaths that they would not meddle with one another's work or finish what another had begun, and also that they had determined how much work they would do in a day and what hours and times they would work. The statute provided that artificers who combined to force certain arbitrary conditions upon employers should be severely punished by the justices in sessions. For the first offence, there was a penalty of £10 or imprisonment; for the second £20 or pillory; and for the third, £40 or pillory, the loss of an ear and infamy.[4] Like the poor laws, the labor statutes culminated in a comprehensive measure under Elizabeth.[5] This act was a revision, extension, and partial codification of the previous laws, and a

[1] 11 Henry VII., c. 22.

[2] 6 Henry VIII., c. 3.

[3] 6 Henry VIII., c. 7.

[4] 2 and 3 Edward VI., c. 15.

[5] 5 Elizabeth, c. 4. This act supplemented the poor law in completing a system for controlling the employed and unemployed. Cunningham, ii, 38.

short exposition of it is necessary in order to understand how completely the whole industrial system was under the supervision of the justices of the peace. It declared that the previous laws for the regulation of artificers, laborers, servants of husbandry, and apprentices were inefficient, and could not be put into operation "without greatest grief and burden of the poor laborer and hired man." The preamble added, "If the substance of as many of the said laws as are mete to be continued shall be digested and reduced to one sole law, and in the same an uniform order prescribed and limited concerning the wages and other orders for apprentices, servants and laborers, there is yet good hope that it will come to pass that the same law being duly exercised should banish idleness, advance husbandry and yield to the hired person, both in time of scarcity and in time of plenty a convenient proportion of wages." No employer could hire a laborer for less than a term of one year to work in any of the "sciences, crafts, mysteries or arts of clothiers, woollen cloth weavers, tuckers, fullers, clothworkers, sheremen, dyers, hosiers, tailors, shoemakers, tanners, pewterers, bakers, brewers, glovers, cutlers, smiths, farriers, curriers, saddlers, spurriers, turners, cappers, hat-makers, felt-makers, bowyers, fletchers, arrow-head makers, butchers, cooks or millers." Certain persons not having property of the annual value of 40s. were required when requested to engage in some trade or husbandry; servants could not be discharged or leave their positions before the end of the term unless on cause allowed by a justice of the peace; laborers were to do their full duty; the system of apprenticeship was regulated; artificers could be made to work in hay time; the labor of poor women, boys, and girls was compulsory; and in short the whole range of industrial relationships was included, and penalties provided for default. All no doubt was intended to secure honest labor. The hours of work were fixed, and servants could not leave their respective parishes and towns without licenses. The rates of wages were to be ascertained by the justices of the peace in quarter sessions, certified to the Chancery, approved by the Privy Council and proclaimed by the sheriffs. A penalty of £10 was inflicted upon justices absenting themselves without lawful excuse from the sessions in which wages were fixed. Penalties were provided for those who paid and received higher wages than those stipulated. The justices could settle disputes arising between masters and servants as to misusage or neglect of duty. Finally it was enacted that the "justices of the peace in every county, dividing themselves into several limits, and likewise every mayor, or head officer of any city or town corporate shall yearly . . . . by all ways and means as to their wisdoms shall be thought most meet, make special and diligent inquiry of the branches and articles of this statute . . . and where they find any defaults to see the same severely corrected and punished without favor, affection, or malice." [1]

Closely connected with the regulation of wages was the control of prices. Persons refusing to sell wine by the tun or at the assessed prices were to forfeit its value. The justices of the peace were authorised to enter the houses of offenders, sell the wine in question, and retain the pro-

[1] This act was further explained, but not essentially altered, by 39 Elizabeth, c. 12. The provision ordering the determination of wages according to the "plenty or scarcity of the time and other circumstances necessarily to be considered," was but a recurrence to a former practice. *English Historical Review,* ix, 310, 311. On the question of assessment of wages during the sixteenth century, see the 1903 edition of Cunningham, *The Growth of British Industry and Commerce,* ii, 37 ff. Appendix A, iii, 894 contains a valuable bibliography of documents.

ceeds as forfeitures.[1] Stricter provisions were made under Edward VI. "To avoid the great price and excesse of wynes" the justices in quarter sessions were ordered to appoint retailers of wines in all places not corporate, and to hear and determine all matters touching the statute.[2] The justices executed the law fixing the prices of meats,[3] and could assess the value of cattle in case of dispute between butchers and owners.[4] The act of Edward VI. which forbade combinations of laborers and artisans also prohibited similar organizations of victuallers. The preamble runs: "Of late days divers sellers of victuals, not content with moderate and reasonable gain, but minding to take for their victuals so much as list them, have conspired and covenanted together to sell their victuals at unreasonable prices . . . . ." The justices of the peace in sessions were ordered to punish butchers, bakers, brewers, and other tradesmen who conspired to sell their goods at certain fixed prices. Heavy penalties were provided.[5] Strict prohibitions were placed on regrators, ingrossers, and forestallers, and offences could be heard and determined by the justices in quarter sessions.[6] All drovers of cattle, badgers, laders, carriers, buyers, and transporters of corn, grain, butter, and cheese were required to hold licenses issued under the seal of justices in quarter sessions.[7] The exportation of certain grains could be allowed by the justices in quarter sessions whenever cheapness was a hindrance to tillage and could be forbidden when dearth was hurtful to the county.[8]

Along with the general statutes regulating wages and prices there was a great number of measures designed to

[1] 24 Henry VIII., c. 6.
[2] 7 Edward VI., c. 5.
[3] 24 Henry VIII., c. 3.
[4] 25 Henry VIII., c. 1.
[5] 2 and 3 Edward VI., c. 15.
[6] 5 and 6 Edward VI., c. 14.
[7] 5 Eliz., c. 12.
[8] 13 Eliz., c. 13. Cunningham, ii, 55.

control the processes of industry and encourage it. The justices of the peace had the execution of the acts regulating the leather trade,[1] the manufacture of boots and shoes,[2] weaving and dyeing woollens,[3] and the preparation of malt.[4] The acts providing for improvement of the breed of horses,[5] fixing the time for killing calves and weanlings,[6] ordering the preservation of forests,[7] protecting the spawn and fry of eels and salmon,[8] and regulating the sizes of wood and the measures of coal[9] were among the minor statutes under the supervision of the justices. They also punished offenders against the statute designed to encourage home manufactures which required men of the lower classes to wear woollen caps on Sundays and holidays.[10]

The rapid development of enclosures during the Tudor period evidently produced disastrous results throughout the realm.[11] From the political standpoint, the decay of tillage, decrease in settled population, and enhanced prices of commodities brought about by the employment of vast tracts of arable land in sheep-raising, were highly undesirable, and measures were devised for the purpose of checking the evils.[12] In an act of the twenty-fifth year of Henry VIII., complaint was made of the amount of land employed in pasture instead of tillage, and it was declared that the poor were "so discouraged with misery and poverty that they fall daily to

[1] 24 Henry VIII., c. 1; 2 and 3 Edward VI., cc. 9, 11.

[2] *Ibid.*

[3] 3 and 4 Edw. VI., c. 2; 5 and 6 Edw. VI., c. 6.

[4] 2 and 3 Edw. VI., c. 10; 39 Eliz., c. 17.

[5] 32 Henry VIII., c. 13; 33 Henry VIII., c. 5.

[6] 24 Henry VIII., c. 7.

[7] 35 Henry VIII., c. 17.

[8] 25 Henry VIII., c. 7.

[9] 34 and 35 Henry VIII., c. 3.

[10] 13 Eliz., c. 19.

[11] Cunningham, i, 526-541.

[12] In the reign of Henry VII., Parliament recognized the political dangers arising from the economic decay. 4 Hen. VII., c. 16.

theft, robbery, and other inconvenience or pitifully die for hunger or cold." Restrictions therefore were placed on sheep-raising forbidding any one to have more than 2000 sheep under a penalty to be enforced by the justices of the peace.[1] For maintenance and increase of tillage, each parish was required to show as much tilled land as had been under cultivation at any time since 1509, and the justices were instructed to certify presentments made under the act to the chancery.[2] The measures of Henry VIII. and Edward VI. were continued with some alterations under Elizabeth.[3] To protect grain from "choughes, crowes, and rokes," all land holders were required to do their best to destroy these pests. Each parish was ordered to provide a crow net, and farmers were to meet and make measures for the destruction of these nuisances. Takers of crows were entitled to two pence per dozen, to be paid by the land owner. Justices of the peace enforced the statute and heard complaints over payments for dead crows.[4]

To encourage the cultivation of hemp for the purpose of supplying naval stores and employing the poor, an act was passed compelling the sowing of a quarter of an acre of hemp or flax for every sixty acres under cultivation.[5] The justices of the peace enforced this measure as well as those ordering the general consumptio n of fish during Lent. These latter acts were also designed to maintain the

[1] 25 Henry VIII., c. 13.

[2] 5 and 6 Edward VI., c. 5. The justices of the peace assisted the six commissioners appointed in 1548 to make inquests into enclosures in a number of the important midland counties. Strype, *Ecclesiastical Memoirs,* II, ii, 350.

[3] 5 Eliz., c. 2; 39 Eliz., c. 2. They were allowed to lapse for a short period, 1592-1597. Cunningham, ii, 52, 53.

[4] 24 Henry VIII., c. 10.

[5] 24 Henry VIII., c. 4.

shipping and fishing industries for commercial and naval purposes.[1]

§ 6. *Justices of the Peace and Police Control.*

It is difficult to separate the judicial from the administrative work of the justices of the peace. No such distinction was made in the minds of legislators at that time. If a measure pertaining to local government needed execution, it was given to the justices to enforce directly or indirectly. Administrative work often involved judicial powers and vice versa.

Although, compared with the preceding century, the Tudor epoch was one of social peace, it was not without serious disorders arising from the waning forces of the middle ages and from the new elements which accompanied the transition to modern times. The most important work of Henry VII. may be said to have been his legislation directed toward the maintenance of a stricter police control. Even Elizabeth found it necessary to issue a proclamation against retaining.[2]

On account of the lawlessness that marked the opening of the Tudor régime, acts were passed strictly enforcing the duties of the coroners, and, to add efficiency to these laws, justices of the peace were empowered to enquire into the escapes of murderers and to hand certificates of the same to the king in his Bench. They were also given authority to take recognisances for keeping the peace and were ordered to certify such recognisances to the general sessions of the peace so that the party bound could be summoned.

[1] 2 and 3 Edward VI., c. 19. The Council sent out a great number of orders enforcing the due observance of Lent. See *Acts of the Privy Council, passim.*

[2] Strype, *Annals of the Reformation,* iv, supplement, 7.

If the party by non-appearance made default, a record of it was taken and sent with the recognisance to the Chancery, King's Bench, or Exchequer. The statute of Richard III.,[1] empowering every justice of the peace to let prisoners and felons to bail at his own discretion, had given rise to great abuses and a large criminal element had been turned loose upon society "to the great displeasure of the king and the annoyance of his liege people." As a remedy for this grievance, it was enacted that bail should only be taken in the presence of at least two justices, one of the *Quorum*. Moreover the justices were ordered to let to bail only persons mainpernable by law, and the time of each bond was to extend only to the next general sessions or gaol delivery. In addition the justices were required to deliver their certificate of the transaction to the general sessions or gaol delivery on pain of forfeiting £10.[2] This law put a check upon the indiscriminate release of prisoners at the caprice of the individual justices.

Complaints were continually made about the difficulty of securing impartial verdicts from juries on account of their fear or favoritism.[3] A statute made in the eleventh year of Henry VII. recites that, on account of the corruption of jurors and the powerful influence of maintenance, embracery, and favor, it had been impossible to obtain in many cases true bills of indictment from juries of inquest. Consequently it was enacted that the justices of the peace of every county in open sessions, upon information made before them for the king, should have authority to hear and determine without indictments by juries all offences and

[1] 1 Richard III., c. 3.

[2] 3 Henry VII., c. 13; also 1 and 2 P. and M., c. 13.

[3] The Paston letters throw a great deal of light on this common abuse of the period.

contempts, saving treason, murder, felony, and offences involving loss of life and member, committed by any person against the existing statutes.[1] This act which placed so much power in the hands of the justices was not of long duration, however, for it was repealed early in the succeeding reign.[2] In order to correct the old abuses of negligence on the part of communities against which the famous statute of Winchester had been directed, a law was passed in Elizabeth's reign compelling the inhabitants of every hundred in case of default after hue and cry to answer for one-half the loss of the person robbed. Two justices living in the hundred could rate and tax the several towns, villages, parishes, and hamlets for the relief of the person aggrieved and enforce the collection of the sum assessed.[3]

The second group of police measures concerned the old troubles of the fifteenth century: livery, maintenance, and unlawful assemblies. On account of the numerous riots and rebellions to the " feere and drede of the subgettis " a statute was passed ordering that, in case any party or parties had unlawfully raised or led a riot and some person had complained to the justices by bill containing an account of the affair, or the rioters had been duly indicted, the justices before whom such complaint or indictment had been made

[1] 11 Henry VII., c. 3. Hallam, *Constitutional History,* i, 31 says that this " serious innovation had evidently been prompted by the spirit of rapacity, which some honest juries had shown courage enough to withstand," and Gneist arrives at the same conclusion. (*Cons. Hist.,* 465.) Their authority for this conclusion is not apparent, and a study of maintenance might have modified it considerably. The long list of statutes against it shows serious attempts at its repression, and it seems far too hasty to conclude that juries were abolished because they were too honest. Schmidt sees in this act an attempt to transform local officers into dependent royal servants. *Op. cit.,* ii, 711. Consolidated royal power was necessary to crush the local disturbances, which bordered on anarchy. Gneist recognised this, 465.

[2] 1 Henry VIII., c. 6.

[3] 27 Eliz., c. 13.

should issue a proclamation ordering the offenders to appear at the sessions immediately following those in which the notice was given. If the party appeared at the appointed time, the justices were to proceed and determine by inquests according to the course of common law and upon conviction to commit the offenders to prison and assess fines at their discretion. Rioters who failed to appear stood convicted. The justices were also required to bind the offenders to keep the peace thenceforward. In case more than forty persons participated in the riot or it seemed heinous, the justices were to investigate the same and upon conviction of the principals to bind them to appear before the king and his council and also to send a record of the matter to the crown. If the party who entered complaint could not make it good, the justices were authorised to assess the damages and costs against the plaintiff.[1] Later this act and all other riot acts were reenforced. A property qualification of twenty shillings freehold or twenty-six and eight pence copyhold was placed on all jurors summoned to enquire into riots and unlawful assemblies. In case of default of verdict by reason of maintenance and embracery, the justices were to send in the names of all offenders in a certificate which was to have the force of a verdict of twelve men.[2] Parliament under Henry VII. also strictly enforced all acts against retainers and placed a heavy penalty on giving and taking livery and on retaining and being retained.[3] Edward VI. and Mary found it necessary to legislate against unlawful assemblies. Whenever a riot or disturbance of the peace occurred, any justice of the peace could raise a *posse* of citizens and go to the scene of trouble. On reaching the place, the justice was to read the following proclamation:

[1] 11 Henry VII., c. 7.

[2] 19 Henry VII., c. 13.

[3] 19 Henry VII., c. 14.

The king our Sovereign Lord charges and commands all persons being assembled immediately to disperse themselves and peaceably depart to their habitations or to their lawful business upon pains contained in the act lately made against unlawful and rebellious assemblies: and God save the King.

If the rioters refused to disband after this notice, the justice could arrest by violence and force of arms if necessary all participants in the fray. The justice and *posse* were not to be held responsible for any deaths that occurred in the arrest of the offenders.[1] Any person who struck another or drew a weapon to strike another in a church-yard was liable to lose an ear or, if he had no ears, to be branded on the cheek and excommunicated. Justices of the peace in sessions enquired into the execution of the law and punished offenders. Under Mary any person who raised a riot for the purpose of changing any laws for the establishment of religion, or attempting to throw open enclosures, destroy deer, pull down houses, barns, or mills, burn corn or grain, or diminish rents or the prices of victuals was declared a felon. The ringing of bells or raising outcry for the purpose of calling an unlawful assembly, and even lending assistance to rioters were declared felony. The former methods of reading the riot act and using force were continued, and extended. All persons from eighteen to sixty years of age were required to assist when called upon by the justices, and any one who refused could be imprisoned for a year. Copyholders who refused were to lose their copyholds and farmers to forfeit their lands for life to their landlords. A penalty of three months' imprisonment could be imposed upon anyone who wilfully concealed a riot from

[1] 3 and 4 Edward VI., c. 5.

the justices. For the better execution of the law, the statute was to be read in quarter sessions.[1]

A third group of statutes was intended to suppress a certain class of vagrants known as mummers and Egyptians. Mummers and disguised persons prowling around were to be arrested as suspects and vagabonds, committed to gaol for three months without bail, and fined at the discretion of the justices. Keeping and selling visors were forbidden also.[2] An act was passed against Egyptians who were accused of wandering from shire to shire without any craft or merchandise, deceiving the people by telling fortunes, and by other cunning tricks, and committing " heinous felonies and robberies." These offenders were ordered to leave the realm, and justices of the peace could imprison them and confiscate their goods.[3] This act was evidently not effective, for in Mary's reign, it was complained that the Egyptians continued in the realm, " using their old accustomed devilish and naughty practices with such abominable lying as is not in any Christian realm to be permitted." Egyptians who did not leave the kingdom within a month were declared felons.[4]

A fourth group of statutes regulated hunting and unlawful games. The justices were to order the arrest of persons accused of hunting in the night or with painted faces or otherwise disguised, to enquire into all such offences, and to bind offenders over to the sessions.[5] They could hear and determine cases of stealing partridges[6] and the eggs of

[1] 1 Mary, s. 2, c. 12. For documents, see Appendix, Nos. VI, VII, VIII, IX.

[2] 3 Henry VIII., c. 9. This was one of the laws which led to the later vagrancy acts.

[3] 22 Henry VIII., c. 10.

[4] 1 and 2 Philip and Mary, c. 4.

[5] 1 Henry VII., c. 7.

[6] 11 Henry VII., c. 17.

hawks and swans. Several statutes were passed for the prevention of hunting by unqualified persons, as well as for the protection of certain kinds of game. The justices could fine persons convicted of tracking hares in the snow and killing them, and of breaking the law established for the protection of wildfowl.[1]

Finally there may be grouped together a number of statutes bearing on different matters which will serve to illustrate the varied character of the work of the justices of the peace. They could hear cases and fine mayors, bailiffs, and other head officers who failed to execute the laws regulating weights and measures or transgressed any of them.[2] They had authority to compel the acceptance of the legal coin of the realm by mayors, bailiffs, constables, and other minor officials,[3] and to enforce the statute regulating the wearing apparel of the various classes.[4] Murder by poison was a crime for which the convicted person was boiled to death without the benefit of the clergy. The justices in sessions were instructed to enquire into such cases and issue writs for the arrest of offenders, who were to be tried by the justices of assize.[5] A penalty of one year's imprisonment and a fine of £10 could be imposed by the justices on persons who wrote, printed, sang, or spoke "phantastical or false prophecies" to the intent of making rebellions, insurrections, or dissensions. By this and other statutes the justices were virtually given a censorship over press and speech. A number of laws passed during the reigns of Edward I. and Richard II. against spreaders of false news and lies about certain dignitaries were revived, and the justices ordered to enforce them. The preamble of the act com-

[1] 25 Henry VIII., c. 11. [2] 7 Henry VII., c. 3; 11 Henry VII., c. 4.
[3] 19 Henry VII., c. 5. [4] 1 Henry VIII., c. 14; 6 Henry VIII., c. 1.
[5] 22 Henry VIII., c. 9.

plains that "divers and sundry malicious and evil disposed persons, maliciously, seditiously and rebelliously and unnaturally . . . have now of late not only imagined, invented, practised, spoken, and spread abroad divers and sundry false, seditious, and slanderous news, rumors, sayings, and tales against our most dread sovereign lord and king, and against our most natural sovereign lady and queen, ... but have also devised, made, written, printed, published, and set forth divers heinous, seditious, and slanderous writings, rhymes, ballads, letters, papers and books intending and practising thereby to move and stir seditious discord, dissension, and rebellion within this realm." Any person who committed such crimes was given for the first offence the choice between pillory and loss of ears, and 100 marks fine and three months in prison. Penalties were provided for even repeating such slander. Justices of the peace who committed such suspects to prison were in a session of two at least, one of the *Quorum,* to have a jury empanelled and to examine the offenders within ten days from the arrest.[1] The justices were to hear and determine in cases of wilful perjury,[2] unlawful usury,[3] and petty misdemeanors, such as breaking fences, robbing orchards, and despoiling woodlands and gardens.[4]

§ 7. *Justices of the Peace and Ecclesiastical Legislation.*

After the separation of the church from Rome, the justices of the peace took their place beside the parson and ordinary in forcing the framework of the new ecclesiastical constitution upon the somewhat disorganised religious system. The payment of tithes was strictly enjoined. The

[1] 1 and 2 Philip and Mary, c. 3.
[2] 5 Eliz., c. 9.
[3] 13 Eliz., c. 8.
[4] 43 Eliz., c. 7.

justices were ordered to assist the church officers in the execution of the law, and to hand offenders over to the ecclesiastical courts for trial.[1] Two justices had authority, upon order from the ecclesiastical judge before whom such an offender was convicted, to commit him to jail until he found security to the effect that he would carry out the provisions of the sentence.[2] By the statute for extinguishing the authority of the Bishop of Rome, all persons, who by writing, preaching, teaching, or act upheld the jurisdiction of the Roman See were to incur the penalty of *praemunire*. Two justices of the peace, one of the *Quorum*, could enquire into all offences against the act and certify presentments to the King's Bench.[3] Two justices under the degree of baron could be summoned by the ordinary to sit with him in the examination and determination of offences committed against the statute of Henry VIII. for the suppression of Romish books, English translations of the Bible, and public reading of the Scriptures.[4] This act also made it an offence for women, artificers, servants, and laborers, with certain exceptions, to read the English Scriptures. A penalty was imposed upon clergymen preaching contrary to true doctrine and upon all persons refusing to take the sacrament. Under the act for Abolishing Diversity of Opinion, the justices of the peace in sessions were empowered to enquire by jury of all heresies, felonies, and contempts against the statute, and to send the indictments and accusations to the Ecclesiastical Commission.[5] This act was later reformed by a provision that no one should be arraigned for such an offence unless indicted before at least three justices and a jury of twelve men.[6]

[1] 27 Henry VIII., c. 20.

[2] 32 Henry VIII., c. 7.

[3] 28 Henry VIII., c. 10.

[4] 34 and 35 Henry VIII., c. 1.

[5] 31 Henry VIII., c. 14.

[6] 35 Henry VIII., c. 5.

The dogmatic reformation under Edward VI. also called the justices of the peace into requisition. Persons contemning, despising, and depraving the blessed sacrament were to suffer imprisonment and to be fined at the king's will and pleasure. For the execution of this statute, the justices or three at least were to take accusations and information on the oaths of two honest citizens, and to enquire in quarter sessions by the oaths of twelve men into the truth of such accusations. They could examine accusers and witnesses and bind them all over to quarter sessions to give testimony. It was provided however that the justices should require by writ in the king's name the presence of the bishop of the diocese or his chancellor at any sessions where offenders against this law were to be tried.[1] All books and missals other than those provided by royal authority were to be "clerelye and utterly abollished, extinguished forever to be used in the realm," and all images in churches and chapels were to be defaced and destroyed. The justices could hear and determine in all cases arising under this act.[2] The statute providing for uniformity of common prayer and administration of the sacraments placed heavy penalties, to be inflicted by the justices, on all who attended any services other than those prescribed by the Established Church.[3]

Under Mary the justices were used to re-establish and maintain Catholicism. For the protection of Roman forms of worship it was made a punishable offence maliciously to disturb, by word or deed, a priest during his sermon or the celebration of the mass, or to pull down or destroy any

[1] 1 Edward VI, c. 1. [2] 3 and 4 Edward VI., c. 10.

[3] 5 and 6 Edward VI., c. 1. In 1549, the King instructed the justices of Devon to offer pardon to all persons who had refused to accept the Book of Common Prayer if they would return to their duty and allegiance. *Domestic Papers,* 1547-1580, 18.

sacred altar, crucifix, or cross of any church. Offenders were to be arrested by the church wardens and constables and taken before a justice of the peace who upon sufficient evidence could commit them for safe keeping. Within six days, two justices at least were to examine the prisoners and if convinced of their guilt were to bind them over to quarter sessions. Upon repentance and reconciliation, an offender could be released after giving security for good behavior.[1] If an offender escaped from the parish where he had committed an offense against the act, the inhabitants were made liable to a fine of £5 which could be imposed by the justices in sessions.[2]

As Elizabeth's laws against Roman authority and practices made their appearance, the justices of the peace were called upon to assist in the execution. In sessions they were given authority to enquire into all cases of persons accused of maintaining, defending, or extolling, by word or deed, the authority of the Pope in England, and to make presentments of their inquisitions to the Queen's Bench.[3] They were to help in the prevention of the importation of crosses, beads, pictures, and other tokens of the Catholic church, and report all offences to the Privy Council.[4] In the twenty-third year of Elizabeth's reign it was declared treason to influence persons to accept the Roman doctrines and misprision of treason to assist in procuring converts.[5] The justices could enquire into offences against this act. Penalties were provided against those who heard or said mass or failed to attend the Established Church, and the justices could hear and determine all cases except treason and mis-

[1] 1 Mary, s. 2, c. 3. [2] *Ibid.*

[3] 5 Eliz., c. 1. For form of indictment, see Appendix, No. XII.

[4] 13 Eliz., c. 2. [5] 23 Eliz., c. 1.

prision.[1] They were required to report to the Privy Council the presence of any Jesuit, Seminary, or Catholic priest in the realm,[2] and to cause to abjure the kingdom every one who refused to conform to the new religious statutes. By the famous Five Mile Act all persons coming under the intent of the statute were required to certify their true names and residences to the minister or curate of the parish, or to the constable, headborough, or tithing man of the town, who in turn was to deliver them to the justices in quarter sessions to be entered upon the rolls. Two justices could hear the oaths of non-conforming recusants to the effect that they would abjure the realm. Two justices with the assent of the bishop of the diocese could, on sufficient reason, issue to persons confined by the Five Mile Act certificates allowing them to go beyond their limits.[3] The justices were also turned against the dissenters. The act to retain the queen's subjects in obedience, directed against "the wicked and dangerous practices of seditious sectaries and disloyal persons," placed heavy penalties on those who refused to attend the Established Church or resorted to unlawful conventicles. The justices of the peace were to warn offenders and in quarter sessions take their oath to abjure the kingdom.[4]

§ 8. *Justices of the Peace and National Defence.*

The whole Tudor policy favored the decay of the feudal military organisation and the full development of the old militia system which laid the obligation of service upon

[1] For the execution of the first clause, the Council instructed the justices to call before them quarterly all parsons, vicars, curates, and church wardens, and to examine into the execution of the law. *Domestic Papers,* 1591-1594, 158.

[2] 35 Eliz., c. 2. [3] *Ibid.* [4] 35 Eliz., c. 1.

every inhabitant capable of serving.[1] The primary care of Tudor legislation on this subject was the encouragement and development of the county system of general obligation. A statute in the third year of Henry VIII., called to mind the splendid feats of the long-bowmen in the past and complained that, on account of unlawful games, archery had been neglected. All persons under sixty with some exceptions were to use and keep in their houses long bows and arrows. Even children were to be provided with bows and arrows and taught to use them. Statutes against unlawful games were ordered to be put into stricter execution, and justices of the peace were instructed to commit offenders to gaol until they gave sufficient security for their future conduct. Regulations were made for the manufacture of bows and arrows, and the justices were to appoint bowyers. Proclamation of the act was to be made in sessions.[2] The justices could punish deserters from the militia.[3] Under the militia act of Philip and Mary the old graduation of the liability to bear arms according to property was revised, and the justices of the peace supervised the execution of the commissions issued from the chancery ordering the organisation and equipment of the county militia. In quarter sessions they heard and determined cases arising from offences against the act.[4]

Under Henry VIII. there appeared special commissioners known as lieutenants of the king whose duties were the organisation and equipment of the local contingents.[5] Under Edward VI. the lieutenants were used to bring the counties

[1] Gneist, *Constitutional History,* 462; Prothero, *Documents,* cxix.

[2] 3 Henry VIII., c. 3; 6 Henry VIII., c. 2; 6 Henry VIII., c. 13; 33 Henry VIII., c. 6.

[3] 3 Henry VIII., c. 5.

[4] 4 and 5 P. and M., c. 2.

[5] Gneist, *Communalverfassung,* i, 315.

into military order when the Catholic disturbances occurred, and under Philip and Mary these officers received parliamentary sanction.[1] The lords-lieutenant were not merely charged with mustering and organising troops; they were empowered to do all things which pertained to the conservation of the peace, and if necessary to declare and enforce martial law. All justices of the peace and other local officials were commanded to lend all possible assistance to the lords-lieutenant on pain of royal displeasure and liability to answer to the crown for negligence.[2] The commissioners of array could also require the aid of the justices.[3] The large discretionary power of the Privy Council in matters pertaining to military affairs[4] led in practice to the extensive use of the justices in all matters pertaining to national defence. Their powers were practically concurrent with those of the lieutenants, and in the absence of commissions appointing lieutenants, they exercised all the local military functions.[5]

[1] 4 and 5 P. and M., c. 3.

[2] Prothero, *Documents*, 154-156. "And further, we will and command all our Justices of the peace . . . . that they, with their power and servants, from time to time shall be attendant, ... and at the commandment as well of you as of your said deputies . . . ."

[3] *Ibid.*, 157. [4] *Ibid.*, cxxi. [5] On the whole question, see below.

CHAPTER V

Privy Council and Justices of the Peace

The organic unity of the Tudor system is clearly revealed in the relations of the justices of the peace and the Privy Council. The latter body was the primary instrument for central administration of all kinds, for "it was in and through the Council that the absolute monarchy performed its work."[1] Though perhaps in theory limited to the functions which had not been vested in the other regular organs of government,[2] in reality its sphere of authority and action was not defined by law, and it assumed and exercised legislative, judicial, and administrative powers. As members of parliament, the councillors influenced the national law-making body, and at the council-board measures were devised which partook of the character of law.[3] This was a natural outcome of its unlimited ordinance power, though in practice it was not inclined to interfere arbitrarily when the existing statutes sufficed to meet the purposes of state.[4] Besides a general supervision of all courts of law, the Council had an extensive original and appellate jurisdiction which was constantly exercised.[5] Its directive control over foreign, military, financial, and internal affairs was practically absolute.

[1] Prothero, *Documents,* ci. [2] Gneist, *Constitutional History,* 500.

[3] Prothero, cii.

[4] *Acts of Privy Council,* 1558-1570, 248 for example.

[5] Prothero, ciii.

§ 1. *Organisation and Powers of the Privy Council.*

Unfortunately the records of the Privy Council for the century preceding 1540 are confined to a few scanty notices. It is therefore impossible to gain an insight into its regular workings during this period.[1] However, the provisions issued in 1526 for the establishment of a Council indicate the character of its composition and the scope of its work. For the purpose of securing a better consideration of the king's important particular affairs and all matters touching the administration of justice, disorders of the realm, and complaints of the royal subjects, a large number of honorable, expert, and discreet persons especially named was instructed to be in attendance upon his majesty.[2] To provide for a constant transaction of the business, in case of the absence of others, the Bishop of Bath, the Secretary, Sir Thomas More, and the Dean of the Chapel, or two of them at least, were ordered to be continually present and "to apply themselves effectually, diligently, uprightly, and justly in the premises, being every day in the forenoon by ten of the clock at the furthest and in the afternoon at two of the clock, in the king's dining chamber, or in such other place as may be appointed for the Council chamber; there to be in readiness not only in case the king's pleasure shall be to commune or confer with them upon any cause or matter, but also for hearing and direction of poor men's complaints on matters of justice." A large number of councillors was generally at the court and meetings of the entire body were held occasionally for the transaction of business. When the king was out of London, he was accompanied by some of his councillors, while others remained behind to determine upon questions which regularly came up to the centre for consideration.

[1] Nicholas, *Proceedings*, vol. vii, p. i.

[2] *Ibid.*, p. v.

Evidently a Council established by royal order, summoned and dismissed by royal command, and consulted only at will would not possess much independence.[1] It was in reality an instrument of the crown, although of course the *personnel* of the body was an important factor which the crown could not entirely ignore.[2] Both the temper of the king and the position of the Council under Henry VIII. are indicated in the latter's reply to the Yorkshire rebels' complaint that the Council contained too many persons of humble birth.[3] After pointing out that the nobility was fully represented, Henry added that the choice of members of the Council was entirely his own affair, and not that of his subjects, and ordered them not to meddle in matters which did not concern them. The Council was in no way responsible to parliament. It was in reality merely a body of royal advisers whom the king chose to consult. He could withhold the most important matter from their consideration, and when he chose to listen to their opinions he was under no compulsion to pay any attention to them. Foreign policies, war and peace, treaties and alliances, and domestic measures of importance were often determined by the earlier Tudors without even the advice of the Council.[4]

The internal administration, however, is all that especially concerns the subject in hand. As has been indicated, the whole internal system was under the direct and

[1] Nicholas, vii, p. iv.

[2] Especially was this true under Elizabeth. The influence of Wolsey and Cromwell was certainly great, but Henry VIII. was his own minister.

[3] Nicholas, vii, p. iv. Fortescue advised the king to appoint humbler men, because they would be less ambitious and more industrious. Chapter xv.

[4] Brewer, *Henry VIII.*, ii, 53.

constant control of the Council.[1] No matter affecting the state was too insignificant to receive its attention. It sought out sedition and treason with never-failing vigilance, and it pried into the affairs of private parties with the same thoroughness. It was extremely active in the apprehension of all opponents of the royal ecclesiastical policy; preachers were silenced if they questioned the proceedings of the crown in matters religious,[2] and authors and printers were quickly punished for issuing publications of doubtful orthodoxy.[3] The Council did not merely investigate affairs that affected the state directly. It interfered with matters which belonged properly to the ordinary courts, and often dealt out justice summarily without any pretence of a jury trial.[4]

The methods which the Council used to obtain information and carry out its decrees show how completely the affairs of the nation down to the minutest details could be scrutinised by the central government. All local officials were subject to the orders of the Council. It had its spies in every locality; it sent special agents to gather information and make arrests; and it influenced the decisions of the judges in their regular courts.[5] It used the rack to extort confessions; it set offenders in stocks and pillory; and "there are two instances of its having inflicted a barbarous punishment without even the forms of trial."[6] It arrested and imprisoned persons on the slightest suspicion and if the charges were afterward found insufficient, it released them without redress.

[1] Hallam, *Const. Hist.*, i, 246, gives an account of how Burleigh whiled away his leisure hours prying into the state of the realm.

[2] Nicholas, vii, pp. xlix. [3] *Ibid.*, xxxvii.

[4] Objection was raised only against individual councillors using their discretion in judicial matters. Prothero, cxvi, and Hallam, i, 235.

[5] Nicholas, vii, p. xlv. See below for interferences in the decisions of the justices of the peace.

[6] Nicholas, vii, pp. xlvi-xlvii.

The primary local functionaries of this central body were the justices of the peace scattered more or less evenly throughout the realm. In the relations of the two sets of officials, it may be clearly seen how the crown was able to keep such a firm grasp upon the whole system of local government, and to maintain a penetrating and constant surveillance over the entire kingdom. The Council and the justices were in continual communication over questions concerning every phase of local administration. No matter seems to have been too petty for their consideration. The justices executed the special orders of the Council, published the proclamations of the government, formed the media of communication between the centre and the people, sent petitions and letters from private persons to the Council, sometimes with their own endorsements, and made reports on general conditions as well as on special matters concerning their respective localities.[1]

§ 2. *Control of the Justices of the Peace.*

The fundamental requisite for successful government was the harmonious co-operation of the two branches of administration. The first care of the Council, therefore, was to secure justices of the peace orthodox on the prevailing ecclesiastical policy and loyal to the government. This was facilitated in a way by the termination of all commissions on the death of the sovereign, which left the successor free to appoint representatives of the new policy. However, this was of comparatively little importance, for the appointment and removal were wholly within the discretion of the

[1] *Acts of Privy Council* (hereafter A. P. C.), 1554-1556, 161. These general reports were not made regularly, notwithstanding the fact that they were required by the Council.

crown. The central government wanted willing and faithful officers and took precautions to secure them. From the number of lists preserved in the State Papers, it appears that the Council must have been fairly well acquainted with the character of the justices and was thus able to make a discriminating selection.

The government sought to detach the justices from complicating local ties by forbidding the appointment of retainers and servants in the commission.[1] All justices under Elizabeth were compelled to declare their obedience to the acts establishing the new ecclesiastical system.[2] Throughout the realm, the justices assembled and took the required oath. The majority of them accepted the new order without protest. There were two exceptions in Cornwall, three in Herefordshire, two in Hampshire, two in Sussex, one in Devon, and one in Berkshire.[3] Those who refused to yield to the new requirements were put out of office. Justices were even dropped from the commission on account of the recusancy of their wives.[4] A man suspected of favoring the papacy or associating with "a perilous fellow of that faction" was not regarded as fit for the office of justice.[5] Some justices were removed because their bishop said that they did not attend church.[6] The Council was doubtless well informed as to the private opinions of the justices. A bishop who discovered two papists in commission promptly sent their names to the Council,[7] and among the State Papers is a list of fourteen justices in Lancashire,

[1] *Domestic Papers* (hereafter *D. P.*), 1547-1580, 178; 1595-1597, 47.

[2] *D. P.*, 1547-1580, 324.

[3] For complete account, see *D. P.*, 1547-1580, 346-366.

[4] *D. P.*, 1581-1590, 449; Hamilton, Quarter Sessions, 328.

[5] *D. P.*, 1581-1590, 240, 241.

[6] *A. P. C.*, 1575-1577, 233.

[7] *D. P.*, 1547-1589, 183

who were suspected of favoring the Pope, together with the names of their dwelling-places, and the state of their families and tenants.[1]

Having secured loyal justices, the next task of the Council was the maintenance of a direct and intimate control. When the state of the highways and the means of communication are taken into consideration, the extent to which supervision was exercised might well excite the admiration of the most enthusiastic German bureaucrat. The Council had before it the names of the hundreds and other divisions of the several counties of England and Wales and the names of the resident justices and other officers.[2] In Elizabeth's reign, an elaborate scheme for the better enforcement of the laws was devised by the Council. There was little new in the measure, for it made use of methods which were ancient in Edward I.'s day. It ordered the *Custos Rotulorum* in every shire to send to the Council the names of the various divisions, parishes, and limits of the county and of the resident justices of the peace, coroners, and clerks. Upon receipt of the lists, the Council was to choose two or three justices in each division and order these justices to summon before them a coroner, a clerk of the peace, and five substantial men of their hundred including one or two chief constables. When the session was assembled, the justices were to charge the members by articles in writing or print to enquire into the material points of certain important statutes. Copies of the statutes were given to the persons summoned and they were ordered to report offences against them within three weeks or a month. On the day prescribed for the presentments, the justices were to receive the information on any offence made by any two inhabitants in the presence of the five representatives. The

[1] *D. P.*, 1591-1594, 159. [2] *D. P.*, 1547-1580, 478-500, *passim*.

five were to present as much as they thought true and also any offences of which they were themselves cognisant. Those making presentments and giving evidence at sessions or assizes were to have their expenses paid out of the fines. The justices were to order the five representatives, the two informers, and all offenders to appear at quarter sessions where each offence was reviewed and bills of indictment preferred. At the quarter sessions, a special jury was to be summoned and, if found in default, to be bound over to the next assize. If the indictments so made against the offenders were not confessed, they were to be tried before the assize justices or removed to the Queen's Bench or Exchequer by *certiorari* to be tried by *nisi prius* or in any court of record at Westminster. Those giving evidence were to have their expenses paid. The clerk of the peace was instructed to make a double roll in parchment and enter the names of persons convicted or indicted at sessions or assizes and the fines inflicted. One roll was to be sent to the Council, in order that it might discover the extent to which the laws were enforced and punish negligent justices of the peace by putting them out of commission.[1]

The Council was quick to deal with irregularities on the part of the justices, and ready to hear the complaints of individuals against maladministration.[2] It was equally ready to interfere with the processes and decisions of the justices. In 1602 the Council was informed that the county of Northumberland was in disorder and that the law-breakers despised the justices of the peace. The Council at once wrote to the justices and ordered them to go to work and reduce the county to order.[3] One Thomas Chatterton sent

[1] *D. P.*, Addenda, 1566-1579, 20-22. [2] *D. P.*, 1581-1590, 264.

[3] *D. P.*, 1601-1603, 214.

in a complaint that he was liable to be overborne and falsely accused of felony in a coming suit for possession, and the Council instructed the justices concerned to make an impartial trial.[1] An Essex man, by debarring the inhabitants of a village from the chapel, had caused a riot which resulted in the arrest of several people. The Council ordered the justices to inflict only small fines for form's sake as they were not the real offenders.[2] When a Wiltshire justice was charged with misdemeanor in taking examinations, the solicitor general was instructed to investigate the charges.[3] The Council required the county magistrates to be in their proper places discharging the obligations laid upon them. At the opening of Edward VI.'s reign a proclamation was issued charging and commanding the justices of the peace to repair to their dwelling-houses "to put themselves in order and readiness to serve his highness as they and every one of them tender his majestie's pleasure and will answer to the contrary at their uttermost perils."[4] In 1587 the mayor was instructed to find out how many justices of the peace were in London and to certify their names and shires to the Council. Justices who had come up to the city were ordered home "as well to attend their charge and office of justices of the peace as to keep house and hospitalitie for the better releveing of their poor neighbours in this time of comon dearthe and scarcetie throughe the realme."[5] Two years later the justices sojourning in London were ordered by the Lord Keeper in his Star Chamber speech to repair to their respective counties and enforce the law on pain of severe punishment.[6] If the

[1] *A. P. C.*, 1577-1578, 308. [2] *A. P. C.*, 1577-1578, 34.

[3] *A. P. C.*, 1586-1587, 385.

[4] *Troubles Connected with the Prayer-Book of 1549*, p. 43. Camden Society Publications.

[5] *A. P. C.*, 1586-1587, 120. [6] *D. P.*, 1598-1601, 347.

justices were lax in the performance of their duties, they generally received a sharp reminder and admonition from the Council.[1]

It was not by writs and orders alone that the Council sought to direct and discipline the justices in the execution of the law. Assize justices in their visitations to the various localities were charged with looking after justices of the peace who were negligent in their office.[2] The Council for the Welsh marches could punish justices who did not do their duty or exceeded it.[3] On his appointment as lord-lieutenant of Sussex and Surrey, the Earl of Arundel was instructed not to allow any one to be a justice of the peace without taking the oath, to watch the doings of the justices, and not to spare any negligence.[4] The failure of several justices in Lancashire to appear at quarter sessions brought a writ from the Council to the sheriff ordering him to investigate the cause of this negligence and to admonish them not to be remiss in their office at their peril.[5] Justices were sometimes charged with the investigation of maladministration on the part of their colleagues.[6] In an order to the sheriff and justices of Yorkshire calling for a stricter enforcement of certain statutes, the justices were warned: "if any of you shall perceive any of your number being justices of the peace in any of these things negligent, we heartily require you or any of you to advertise us or any of us by your private and secret letters or else to the justices of assize at their coming of this. For in so doing we must allow you and we mean to provide some good remedy as reason it

[1] *A. P. C.*, 1581-1582, 427.

[2] *D. P.*, 1598-1601, 441. This is only a special instance. By virtue of their commission they regularly inquired into the doings of the justices of the peace.

[3] *D. P.*, 1601-1603, 217.

[4] *D. P.*, Addenda, 1601-1603, 495.

[5] *A. P. C.*, 1581-1582, 320.

[6] *A. P. C.*, 1588, 353.

should be to remove the credit and estimation from them that willfully deserve the contrary." [1] In addition to the utilisation of the courts and various means of administrative control, the Council in special cases ordered the refractory justices to appear in London to answer for their conduct.[2] For example, Sussex justices who did not exercise the proper care in selecting and arming soldiers for the continental service in 1589 were commanded to appear before the Privy Council to answer for their negligence.[3] On one occasion, the justices of Staffordshire were ordered to make special inquiry into a riot at Drayton Basset but failed to obey their instructions. They were promptly commanded to appear before the Council to account for their disobedience.[4] Two justices accused of uttering slanderous rhymes were called before the Council and soundly rated for setting such a bad example and disgracing their office.[5] As has been pointed out, the Court of Star Chamber had jurisdiction over all offences on the part of officials.[6] Notwithstanding all these precautions and methods, it cannot be doubted that the execution of the law was lax when viewed in the light of modern administration.

§ 3. *The Council and Justices at Work.*

As a rule the orders and instructions issued to the justices of the peace by the Council were specific, relating to parti-

[1] Strype, *Annals of the Reformation,* i, Appendix, 87.

[2] This was also the customary practice in regard to juries charged with corruption and misdemeanors. Smith, *The Commonwealth of England,* ed. 1589, Bk. III, c. 1. Prothero, 180.

[3] *A. P. C.,* 1589-1590, 166.

[4] *A. P. C.,* 1578-1580, 203; *A. P. C.,* 1580-1581, 246.

[5] *A. P. C.,* 1571-1575, 387.

[6] See Carew's Case, Moore, *Reports,* 1512-1621, p. 628. Nota que Carew justice de peace de Devon fuit censure, &c. Scofield, *A Study of the Court of Star Chamber,* p. xv.

cular affairs, but sometimes they were general and addressed to all magistrates throughout the realm. For instance, in 1538 a circular was sent to the justices thanking them for what they had done in the execution of the king's previous letters, directing them to maintain the king's supremacy and to hand over those who supported the Bishop of Rome. They were ordered to punish spreaders of seditious rumors, to expel and correct vagabonds and valiant beggars, to keep watches for these purposes, and to administer justice indifferently. It was stated that several of the justices of the peace had done their duty so well that the king's subjects had not been disquieted for a long time until of late some ungracious persons had endeavored to seduce them with lies and untrue rumors. The chief offenders seem to have been the parsons, vicars, and curates who "read so confusely, hemming and hacking the Word of God and such our injunctions as we have lately set forth that no man can understand the true meaning of the said injunctions." "These miserable and superstitious wretches," calling to mind the struggle of Becket and Henry II., had raised old rumors to promote a new commotion. Justices were consequently enjoined to use their utmost diligence in finding out such "cankered parsons, vicars and curates who do not substantially declare our injunctions but mumble them confusely saying that they have been compelled to read them and bidding their parishens nevertheless to do as they did in times past." The justices were to find out seditious taletellers and commit them to prison without bail to await the justices of assize.[1] Another letter to the justices of the peace expressed surprise that, notwithstanding the sundry advertisements lately made to them to do their duty, things had not been directed with any regard to the "good moni-

[1] *Letters and Papers of Henry VIII.*, vol. xiii, part 2, no. 1171.

tions" set forth for the advancement of justice. They were warned of the dangers they incurred by their negligence and commanded to have special regard for the following points: 1. "the king having expelled the usurped power of the Bishop of Rome with all its branches and dependents desires that privy maintainers of that papistical faction be tried out as the most cankerous and venemous worms in the commonwealth, enemies to God and traitors; 2. raisers and spreaders of bruits touching the king and his honor or security, the state of the realm or the mutation of any law or customs are to be punished; 3. sturdy vagabonds and valiant beggars are to be punished according to the late statute the neglect of which has spread no small inconvenience . . . Unlawful games are to be suppressed and every man is to use the long bow as the law requires; 4. the justices of the peace shall earnestly bend themselves to the advancement of justice between party and party that good subjects may have the benefit of the laws and evil doers be punished." The king trusts that this "gentle admonition" will stimulate them to atone for past remissness, but if any neglect it "the next advice shall be of so sharp a sort as shall bring with it a just punishment on those that shall be found offenders in this behalf." [1] This slight glimpse into the dynamics of the "reformation" gives some indication of the fuller understanding of that great movement which would be possible if the local records of the time were only forthcoming. How much local activity these "gentle admonitions" caused is a matter for conjecture, but we may well imagine that the central government was by no means lax in forcing its measures into execution.

In general, the communications between the Council and the justices pertained to questions of police and administra-

[1] *Letters and Papers,* vol. xvi, no. 945, 1541.

tion which were dealt with in the statutes, but from time to time supplementary orders and proclamations were issued. Only a detailed and perhaps tedious study of these orders and instructions will yield the concrete facts necessary to a proper understanding of the methods and operations of Tudor government. The documents are of such a varied character that they do not lend themselves readily to generalisation, but they do fall into certain broad divisions.

Ecclesiastical. Amid the religious changes of this epoch, two general tasks confronted each government: the enforcement of the new order and the repression of dissent. It need scarcely be remarked that the execution of these tasks occupied a large share of the government's attention during the epoch under consideration. The statutes, however, covered the ground quite thoroughly and provided penalties for offenders. Against Catholics and Puritans alike, the justices were instructed to maintain the establishment, but the enforcement of the law seems to have varied with the great movements which were regarded as dangerous to the state and crown. Whenever political danger was apprehended, a more rigorous execution of the law could easily be brought about by issuing orders to the justices. The prominent recusants were constantly under the eyes of the government, and various expedients were adopted from time to time to keep the Council informed of their doings. In 1582, the sheriffs and justices of the peace were instructed to make reports of the recusants who had been indicted and those at liberty under bond.[1] In order to expedite matters, the Council had a list of all Jesuits, priests, and recusants arranged in alphabetical order.[2] This list was kept complete by the regular information sent in by the justices. In 1592, the Council ordered them to forward schedules of

[1] *D. P.*, 1581-1590, 58.

[2] *D. P.*, 1581-1590, 354.

resident recusants, to visit the houses of such offenders, seize their arms, and certify their yearly revenues and the value of their goods.[1] Three years later, the Archbishops of Canterbury and York were instructed to ascertain by inquest the number of recusants in each parish, their state and degree, how many were resident householders, what means had been take to reform them by instruction, how many had been indicted by law, and what penalties they had paid. In the execution of this order, the bishops were instructed to confer with the "well devoted" justices of the peace in their respective jurisdictions.[2] The justices had a regular certificate for recusants who had not repaired to church for twelve months.[3] Recusancy was an important source of revenue which the Crown did not neglect. In 1585, the Council informed the sheriffs and justices that Her Majesty was graciously pleased on account of the readiness with which the recusants had furnished light horse for her service, and accordingly would grant them immunity from the pains and penalties inflicted by law on condition that they would offer a reasonable annual compensation.[4] In response to instructions from the Council the justices went into the whole matter, and sent in lists of those willing to make the required compensation. Sometimes the offers of the recusants were made over their own signatures. One offered five marks annually and another £100 for the dispensation.[5] Later in the same year loud complaints went up that papists were living at their ease.[6] The justices of the peace were also used by the High Commission and in-

[1] *D. P.*, 1591-1594, 300.

[2] *D. P.*, 1595-1597, 129.

[3] *D. P.*, 1581-1590, 59.

[4] *D. P.*, 1581-1590, 307.

[5] *Ibid.*, 313, 315, 318, 319, 321, 322, 323, 325, 327, 330.

[6] *Ibid.*, 361.

structed to lend all possible assistance as they cherished the queen's pleasure and at their peril for negligence.[1]

In addition to the general measures applying to the whole realm, the Council was informed by different means of the conditions of the various parts, and issued instructions to the justices accordingly.[2] A resident of Berkshire refused to have his child baptised and another condemned the rejoicings at the discovery of the late treason (1586) and harbored papists. The justices promptly informed the Council of these two offenders. The house of the latter was searched, his servants examined, and bonds for his appearance taken.[3] The justices even used torture to wring information from recusants.[4] Some Suffolk justices informed the Council of the apprehension of an offender who had expressed an evil opinion against the sacrament, and received instructions as to procedure.[5] These examples fairly illustrate the character of the work which the justices did in matters ecclesiastical.[6]

[1] Prothero, *Documents*, 232.

[2] *D. P.*, 1591-1594, 158. The High Commission was also an important source of information.

[3] *D. P.*, 1581-1590, 351.

[4] *D. P.*, 1591-1594, 297.

[5] *A. P. C.*, 1542-1547, 417.

[6] The Sussex and Devon justices were ordered to apprehend unlicensed preachers. *A. P. C.*, 1558-1570, 65, 92. Under Mary, the Sussex magistrates were ordered to be more diligent in punishing evil-disordered persons who "railed upon the mysteries of Christ's religion." *A. P. C.*, 1554-1556, 61. The Norfolk justices were instructed to discharge two servants from their employer's service because they did not attend church, and to warn all persons against employing religious suspects. *A. P. C.*, 1577-1578, 316. The Berkshire justices were thanked for their zeal against recusants. *A. P. C.*, 1586-1587, 215. The justices in Gloucestershire were ordered to examine into alleged abuses of the registrar of Gloucester, and send information to the Archbishop of Canterbury of matters belonging to the High Commission. *A. P. C.*, 1586-1587, 39.

The Council and justices were especially active in the apprehension of Jesuits and priests. In 1578, orders were sent to all magistrates instructing them to arrest all priests going about disguised.[1] When they captured such offenders, they sometimes sent them to London under sure guard and forwarded their books, papers, and the records of the preliminary examinations.[2] Justices along the coast took precautions to examine passengers coming from abroad and those seeking to leave the realm.[3]

The non-conformists were also under the close surveillance of the justices. The Leicestershire magistrates reported to the Council that they had discovered "a secte of disordered personnes using to assemble together nere unto a woodside, appointing unto themselves a minister and a private order of service according to their own fantasies." The justices were thanked for their precaution and instructed to take the offenders before the bishop of the diocese to be reduced to conformity.[4] A Suffolk justice reported the "disorders of a dangerous secte termed Family of Love," and the bishop of Norwich was informed of the affair by the Council.[5]

Regulation of Prices. It was a part of the economic policy of the time to prevent speculation in food-stuffs and to maintain "reasonable" prices. In order to carry out this policy on a national scale, the Council and justices had to keep in constant and systematic co-operation. Owing, however, to the immobility of capital and labor and the local character of most of the trade, the control was in a large measure a matter for the various shires. The general policy

[1] *A. P. C.*, 1577-1578, 317.

[2] *A. P. C.*, 1542-1547, 234; *Ibid.*, 1577-1578, 348; *D. P.*, 1581-1590, 237.

[3] *D. P.*, 1591-1594, 465.

[4] *A. P. C.*, 1577-1578, 427.

[5] *Ibid.*, 1578-1580, 139, 445. Willingness to conform was sometimes acknowledged at open sessions. *D. P.*, 1581-1590, 321.

in the regulation of prices was carried out by obtaining a knowledge of the amount of commodities in existence at a given time and making a comparison with the state of the markets. If there was a scarcity, exportation was restricted,[1] and farmers were compelled to bring their grain to market. In the times of abundance, exportation was allowed. The gathering of this information and the execution of this policy were in the main the work of the justices of the peace under the supervision of the Council, although special commissions were sometimes issued for the "view" of grain, in which the justices assisted.[2] From time to time instructions were sent out to the justices ordering them to regulate grain, to search granaries, supply the markets, and apprehend regrators and forestallers.[3] An excellent example of the thoroughness of the work of the justices is given in a report from Norfolk which contains not only an account of their proceedings in supplying the markets, but also a certificate of the "whole sum and quantity of grain and the names of the owners in the several hundreds."[4]

If the prices of grain went too high, the justices were ordered to bring them down and to restrain badgers.[5] In cases of great dearth, various expedients were resorted to. In 1577, the justices of Cumberland petitioned the Council for relief owing to the great corn famine there. The Lord Keeper was instructed to report on the state of that county

[1] *D. P.*, 1547-1580, 449; *A. P. C.*, 1578-1580, 208, 222.

[2] *A. P. C.*, 1542-1547, 259.

[3] *D. P.*, 1547-1580, 26; *Ibid.*, 1581-1590, 328. In 1586, the justices were ordered to "reform" the disorders of farmers in not supplying the markets in times of dearth. *A. P. C.*, 1586-1587, 119. The orders made by the justices of a Warwickshire hundred for the restraint of high prices, to be observed in all parishes, are preserved in *D. P.*, 1581-1590, 391.

[4] *D. P.*, 1581-1590, 338.

[5] *A. P. C.*, 1575-1577, 219.

and to see what relief was needed.[1] In a time of scarcity in Gloucestershire, the justices were instructed to appoint assistants, search barns, find out the store of each farmer, and furnish the markets at "reasonable and convenient" prices. They were, however, cautioned to "proceed with such good discretion as there shall grow no disorder or inconvenience thereby." [2] If any refused to obey the Council's instructions, the justices were to take their bonds and order them to appear in London to answer for contempt. In 1586, the justices of Devonshire informed the Council that, owing to the high prices of grain, the poor were in danger of perishing, but that many vessels laden with grain for exportation were in the Devon harbors. The Council instructed them to attach the ships, sell the grain according to "equity and justice" and make due compensation to the owners.[3]

Wages and Industry. The regulation of wages was provided for by statutes, and practically the only notices on the question which occur in the Acts and Papers are orders made for the printing of rates sent in by the justices according to law.[4] The acts controlling the methods and processes of industry were occasionally supplemented by orders and instructions from the centre.[5]

Relief of the Poor. Several excellent examples of the direct utilisation of industry for the purpose of employing the

[1] *A. P. C.*, 1577-1578, 181. [2] *A. P. C.*, 1586-1587, 71, 72.

[3] *A. P. C.*, 1586-1587, 59-60. The justices in Beds, Herts, and Bucks were ordered to post the names of badgers in the county towns, so that all might know who was appointed and for how long. *A. P. C.*, 1571-1575, 197. For the regulation of the prices of other commodities, see *D. P.*, 1547-1580, 30, 31. On prices of cattle, *A. P. C.*, 1550-1552, 366; butter and cheese, *ibid.*, 376; victuals, *ibid.*, 135, 137, 140.

[4] *A. P. C.*, 1581-1582, 132; 1586-1587, 187; 1588, 168. *English Historical Review*, xv, 445.

[5] *D. P.*, *Addenda*, 1601-1603, 404; *A. P. C.*, 1589-1590, 8; *ibid.*, 1570-1580, 168; *ibid.*, 1581-1582, 309.

poor are to be found in the papers. In 1586, the Council was informed that "the poorer sort of people inhabiting about the city of Bath and other towns in the easterly part of the county of Somerset wont to live by spining, carding and workeing of wolle" were not set to work, and, owing to the dearth of corn and victuals, were in need of the necessities of life—"a matter not onlie full of pitie in respect of the people but of dangerous consequence to the state if speedie order be not taken therein." The justices and sheriff were therefore ordered to assemble and devise a method of remedying the evil. They were authorised to summon before themselves the clothiers and other men of trade in the various places where there were complaints of want of employment and in Her Majesty's name to command each of them who had stocks and ability, to employ workmen, as they had done previously so that the poor would find relief. The justices were to send to the Council the names of those who refused to obey and their excuses for their conduct.[1] The justices were required to ascertain the number of acres to be sown in the various counties so that the poor could be well employed.[2]

Highways. The regular statutes providing for the maintenance of highways and bridges were occasionally supplemented by orders from the Council in special cases, but as a rule there was a strong inclination to observe the law as laid down by Parliament. When the justices of Huntingdon county asked the Council for permission to collect a benevolence for the repair of the great bridge at Huntingdon, the latter replied that the request could not be granted for the reason that there was a statute providing for such contingencies and that it could not be arbitrarily broken.[3]

[1] *A. P. C.*, 1586-1587, 93; *ibid.*, 1587-1588, 200, 265.

[2] *A. P. C.*, 1586-1587, 8.

[3] *A. P. C.*, 1558-1570, 248.

To aid in the construction of the harbor at Dover, the Council ordered the justices in every shire to levy a fine of two shillings and sixpence on every ale-house license.[1] The justices in the eastern counties were required to collect contributions toward the expenses of draining the Fens.[2] The establishment and maintenance of beacons and guard along the coast were duties of which the justices were frequently reminded by the Council.[3]

Care of Defectives and Public Health. The special care of lunatics and idiots does not seem to have attracted any attention from the state. Where they were dependent, they were doubtless included among the ordinary paupers in the county charge. There is one instance of the justices making an examination of a man who appeared to be "distempered in his wits." The Council wrote to a dean instructing him to see if the man could be reduced to order by "counsel or phisike" or should be placed in the care of his friends.[4] In the time of plague the justices did the work of a health committee.

Police Control. The police measures of the Council reenforced rather than extended the powers which the statutes conferred upon the justices of the peace. Smith, in his *Commonwealth,* gives a full description of the methods adopted to ensure a thorough policing of the realm:

And commonly every year or each second year in the beginning of summer or afterwards (for in warm time the people for the most part be more unruly) even in the calm time of peace, the Prince with his Council chooseth certain articles out of penal laws already made for to repress the pride and evil rule of the popular, and sendeth them down to the justices willing them to look upon those points and after they have met

[1] *D. P.,* 1547-1580, 649.

[2] *A. P. C.,* 1575-1577, 134.

[3] *D. P.,* 1547-1580, 7, 8, *passim.*

[4] *A. P. C.,* 1578-1580, 100.

together and consulted among themselves how to order that matter most wisely and circumspectly whereby the people might be kept in good order and obedience after the law, they divide themselves by three or four and so each in his quarter taketh order for the execution of the said articles. And then within certain space, they meet again and certify the Prince or his Privy Council how they do find the shire in rule and order touching those points and all other disorders. There was never in any Commonwealth devised a more wise, a more dulce and gentle, nor a more certain way to rule the people, whereby they are always kept as it were in a bridle of good order and sooner looked into that they should not offend than punished when they have offended. . . So that it is as a new furbishing of the good Lawes of the Realm and continual repressing of Disorders which do naturally rest among men.[1]

The documents contain a large number of orders from the Council designed to secure a better enforcement of the laws against vagabonds, rioters, and spreaders of seditious rumors,[2] and instructing the justices as to the best methods of proceeding to maintain social order. The justices also had a large amount of police work of a varied character. They were required to assist in the apprehension of prisoners escaped from Marshalsea;[3] to repress revolts in the making,[4] to repress idlers of all kinds;[5] to collect money

[1] Smith, *Commonwealth,* 164-166.

[2] In 1571, the Council required the justices to take extra precautions in the apprehension of rogues, and to send in certificates of those punished in the various hundreds. *D. P.,* 1547-1580, 440. The justices of the counties around London were ordered to meet and devise some method of ridding the suburbs of rogues. *A. P. C.,* 1587-1588, 256. In 1591, the lords-lieutenant were instructed to use martial law on the vagabonds, and to specially direct the justices in the execution of the law. *D. P.,* 1591-1594, 120. The justices in sessions issued orders to the local officers instructing them in the apprehension of vagrants. *D. P.,* 1581-1590, 51.

[3] *A. P. C.,* 1577-1578, 292.

[4] *Ibid.,* 1552-1554, 426.

[5] *Ibid.,* 1542-1547, 467.

and reimburse gaolers for the support of prisoners; [1] to make special enquiries into important murder cases; [2] to punish the spreaders of false rumors against the queen; [3] to arrest and punish pirates; [4] to keep order at fairs and wakes; [5] to examine embezzlers and report to the Council; [6] to examine maimed beggars and relieve *bona fide* soldiers; [7] to restore estates seized by force; [8] and to assist in the search for pirates' plunder. [9]

Military and Naval Obligations. The justices of the peace proved to be efficient officers for recruiting, equipping, drilling, and maintaining soldiers, for securing and transporting supplies for the army and navy, and for guarding the coasts in times of apprehended danger. In this work they sometimes co-operated with the lords-lieutenant and sometimes did the whole of it by themselves. [10] The number of soldiers for a given undertaking was apportioned among the shires and letters sent to the justices of each to levy their quota. [11] They assisted the commissioners assigned to impress soldiers and sailors, and imprisoned, to await the Lord Admiral's pleasure, those who refused to obey orders. [12] The justices of Kent furnished horses and messengers for the service between London and Dover, and forwarded victuals ordered to the latter port. [13] The justices made provisions for assessing and collecting the money for equipments, [14] and superintended the disbursement of the same. [15] They arrested offenders against the muster offi-

[1] *A. P. C.*, 1581-1582, 278.
[2] *Ibid.*, 1542-1547, 173.
[3] *Ibid.*, 1550-1552, 50.
[4] *D. P.*, 1547-1580, 532.
[5] *A. P. C.*, 1554-1556, 162.
[6] *Ibid.*, 1556-1558, 94.
[7] *Ibid.*, 1586-1587, 253.
[8] *Ibid.*, 1550-1552, 414.
[9] *Ibid.*, 1588, 385.
[10] *D. P.*, 1581-1590, 175.
[11] *Ibid.*, 1547-1580, 582.
[12] *A. P. C.*, 1556-1558, 238.
[13] *Ibid.*, 236.
[14] *D. P.*, 1547-1580, 343, 374, 376, 377, *passim.*
[15] *Ibid.* and *A. P. C.*, 1586-1587, 388.

cers,[1] and supplied beef,[2] lumber,[3] hemp,[4] and provisions,[5] to the navy. They also assisted in the equipment of ships for the apprehension of pirates.[6]

The justices were particularly active in the preparations for the expected Spanish invasion.[7] They viewed the ports and landing places,[8] and reported conditions to the Council. Any person who observed the approach of a fleet of more than ten ships was required to inform the nearest justice who was in turn to take immediate action for defense.[9] The justices were also required to assist in guarding against Scotch inroads.[10]

Purveyance. This old grievance was the source of some difficulty under the Tudors notwithstanding the statutes regulating it. The whole matter was practically under the control of the justices so far as local arrangements were concerned. If the inhabitants of a hundred refused to furnish the supplies required of them, the justices were to exert compulsion under order from the Council.[11] In a general way the justices were in charge of the supply apportioned to each county by the Lord Steward,[12] and occasionally made composition for their quota. In 1586, the justices in all counties were instructed to make diligent inquiry into all debts owing in the several parishes by default of the Royal Purveyor and to ascertain to whom the amounts were owing in order that the Council could settle complaints.[13]

[1] *A. P. C.*, 1571-1575, 194.
[2] *Ibid.*, 1589-1590, 390.
[3] *Ibid.*, 1571-1575, 124.
[4] *Ibid.*, 1575-1577, 343.
[5] *Ibid.*, 1556-1558, 70.
[6] *Ibid.*, 1558-1570, 164.
[7] *A. P. C.*, 1558, 119, 145, 161, 188, 281, 232, 243, *passim.*
[8] *D. P.*, 1581-1590, 349.
[9] *A. P. C.*, 1556-1558, 402.
[10] *Ibid.*, 1547-1550, 471.
[11] *D. P.*, 1540-1580, 250.
[12] *A. P. C.*, 1542-1547, 160. See also Hamilton, *Quarter Sessions.*
[13] *A. P. C.*, 1586-1587, 45.

Miscellaneous. The varied character of the justices' work is illustrated by a general collection of orders from the Council. The justices settled quarrels over domestic servants,[1] assisted in the recovery of wrecked goods,[2] issued licenses to persons wishing to dig for treasure,[3] took collections for redeeming mariners seized by the Turks,[4] helped to protect debtors against rapacious creditors,[5] and enforced the payment of the "loan" of 1589.[6] They also issued permits to beg and collect benefits for those who suffered losses by fire and at sea.[7] These examples will serve to illustrate the miscellaneous duties discharged by the justices. They might be multiplied indefinitely, for the Tudor system was highly inquisitorial and there was absolutely no sphere of individual immunity, in theory or practice, from government interference.

[1] *A. P. C.*, 1575-1578, 381.
[2] *Ibid.*, 1577-1578, 183.
[3] *D. P.*, 1595-1597, 148.
[4] *A. P. C.*, 1578-1580, 193.
[5] *Ibid.*, 1588-1589, 24.
[6] *Ibid.*, 1588-1589, 165, 264.
[7] *D. P.*, 1591-1594, 128, 144, 187, 136, *passim*.

CHAPTER VI

THE CONSTITUTION OF THE OFFICE OF JUSTICE OF THE PEACE

Appointment. There is considerable indefiniteness as to the exact method followed in the selection and commissioning of the justices and doubtless there was not a little variation in practice. An act of Richard II. provided that the Chancellor, Treasurer, Keeper of the Privy Seal, Steward of the King's House, the King's Chamberlain, Clerk of the Rolls, Justices of the Benches, Barons of the Exchequer and all others having the power to appoint justices of the peace or other royal officers should take an oath that they would not be influenced by favor or prejudice.[1] Whether these high officials acted together or separately in appointing justices is not apparent in the statute. Moreover it may have been a temporary measure.[2] By an act of Henry V. the justices were to be appointed by the advice of the Chancellor and the King's Council, and vacancies caused by want of property qualifications could be filled by the Chancellor.[3] The statute creating justices of the peace in Wales placed the power of appointment in the hands of the Lord Chancellor or the Lord Keeper of the Great Seal. It may be safely concluded that the Chancellor exercised a large discretion, but various expedients were devised for obtain-

[1] 12 Ric. II., c. 2.

[2] Lambard, *Eirenarcha*, ed. 1602, 26.

[3] 2 Henry V., s. 2, c. 1; 18 Henry VI., c. 11.

ing information as to persons best fitted for the commission. They were appointed at the suggestion of the Council,[1] of local magnates,[2] and of justices of assize,[3] and in Wales the resident Council seems practically to have selected the justices for the western counties.[4] In some corporations the mayor and recorder were *ex officio* justices of the peace, and in one or two special instances local dignitaries by royal grant had the power of assigning justices.[5] The small ambitions of local gentlemen led them to seek appointment and to bring themselves to the notice of the Chancellor by various means. A speech of Mr. Glascock in an Elizabethan parliament gives a glimpse into the county politics of the time:

Then let us see whence these justices do come, and how they be made. It cannot be denied but all justices are made by the Lord Keeper; then he is at fault and no one else. . . . . No, I may more easily excuse him than ourselves, for he maketh none but such as have certificates commendatory from the justices of assize. Why, then, they be in fault; for impossible it is that my Lord Keeper should know the quality and efficiency of them himself, but only *per alium* in trust as by the justices of assize. No, the gall lies not there for they neither (by reason that they are not always riding in one circuit) are well acquainted with the nature of those justices; but when any desireth to be a justice he geteth a certificate from divers justices of the peace in the country to the justices of assize certifying of their sufficiency and ability. And they again maketh their certificate (believing the former) to the Lord Keeper who at the next assizes puts them into commission. And thus is the Lord Keeper abused and the justices of assize

[1] *A. P. C.*, 1580-1581, 67.
[2] *Ibid.*, 1587-1588, 302.
[3] *D. P.*, 1547-1580, 178.
[4] *A. P. C.*, 1575-1577, 346.
[5] *Beverley Town Documents*, Selden Society, 67.

abused and the country troubled with a corrupt justice put in authority.[1]

Service was compulsory and could be avoided only by a special patent of exemption.[2] This was not issued often, however, for, although the office was an undesirable one from the point of view of compensation, it was extremely useful to the rising middle class which sought political influence and economic control.

The Commission of the Peace.[3] Justices of the peace acquired their office and powers from a commission issued from the chancery. By the time of Elizabeth, this commission had grown to such a bulk by the constant increase of statutes conferring additional powers upon the justices that considerable confusion existed. It was moreover filled with errors from repeated rewriting and the failure of the clerks to cut out obsolete acts. Lambard, in the early editions of his work, laid great stress upon the necessity for reform in the commission and it was finally accomplished in the Michaelmas term of 1590. Christopher Wray, the Chief Justice, Sir Edmund Anderson, Chief Justice of the Common Pleas, Sir Roger Manwood, Chief Baron of the Exchequer, and other judges and barons held a conference,

[1] *Parliamentary History*, i, 953-954.

[2] *D. P.*, 1594-1597, 48; *Calendar of Patent Rolls*, 1476-1485, 53.

[3] In Henry VI.'s day, commissions of the peace were issued for Beds, Berks, Bucks, Cambridgeshire, Cambridge town, Cornwall, Cumberland, Derbyshire, Devon, Dorsetshire, Essex, Gloucestershire, Hampshire, Herefordshire, Herts, Huntingdonshire, Kent, Leicestershire; Holland, Kesteven, and Lindsey, in Lincolnshire; Middlesex, Norfolk, Town of Lynn, Great Yarmouth, Northamptonshire, Northumberland, Notts, Oxfordshire, Oxford town, Rutland, Shropshire, Somersetshire, Staffordshire, Suffolk, Ipswich town, Surrey, Sussex, Warwickshire, Westmoreland, Wiltshire, Worcestershire; and North, East, and West Ridings, in Yorkshire. *Calendar of Patent Rolls*, 1422-1429, 559-573.

revised the commission, cast out extraneous matter and the obsolete statutes and drew up a new form which they submitted to Sir Christopher Hatton, Lord Chancellor, who, approving the draft, ordered it to supersede the old commission.[1] "So the great charter, if it may so be called, of the authority and power of the justices of the peace was conceived in terms of general and intelligible import, setting forth at large the general trusts imposed in them, whether to prevent, inquire or punish."[2] This new form of the commission is now to be examined.

After the usual greeting of the queen to those appointed to be justices of the peace, came an enumeration of their powers and duties. They were assigned jointly and severally to conserve the peace in their county, to enforce and to cause to be enforced all ordinances and statutes *pro bono pacis nostrae*—which Lambard interpreted to mean the statutes of Westminster, all laws and statutes made for arresting robbers, murderers, felons, and suspected criminals, and for the repression of riots, affrays, violence, and the disturbance of public peace.[3] This first clause also gave the justices power to punish transgressors against the statutes and to take bail for the keeping of the peace.

The second clause contained instructions for the sessions. Two or more justices, one of whom was to be of the *Quorum,* were to enquire *per sacramentum proborum et legalium hominum* into a long list of offences against the statutes, and also into the negligence of officials. They were also to hear and determine in cases of indictment, and to assess fines and order the punishment of the convicted.

[1] Reeves, *History of English Law,* v, 228.

[2] *Ibid.,* v, 228. The old and new commissions are published in Prothero's *Statutes and Constitutional Documents,* 144-149. For the new commission, see Appendix I, below.

[3] Lambard, *Eirenarcha,* 43.

The third clause contained a provision that in cases of doubt and difficulty the justices of the peace were not to proceed unless there should be present one of the justices of the King's Bench, or at least one of the justices of assize.

Then followed the charge to the justices that they should diligently carry out the duties given to them in the preceding clauses, especially saving to the queen *amerciamentis et aliis ad nos spectantibus*.

The final clause contained instructions to the sheriff and *Custos Rotulorum*. The former was commanded to return the jury upon certain days and at certain places which the justices of the peace should designate, and the latter was to keep the records of writs, proceedings, and indictments. As soon as a commission was directed out of the chancery a *dedimus potestatem* was directed to some acting or "ancient justices of the peace" or some other important official to take the oath of the persons to whom the commission was addressed.[1] By the first oath the justice was sworn to do equal right to rich and poor, to execute the statutes of the realm without prejudice, to make honest returns of fines and amerciaments, and to take no unlawful fees. The second oath was that of Supremacy required of all officials.

[1] By an order of the Privy Council, justices of assize were authorised to administer the oaths. *Acts*, 1578-1580, 178. A letter to the justices of the peace in Devon from the Lords of the Council "begins by reciting that the Queen's Majesty has been informed that some persons exercise the office of justice of the peace without taking the necessary oaths, and it is difficult to distinguish those who have done so from those who have not; so her pleasure is that all justices, without prejudice, should immediately take them. Copies of the oaths and a writ of *dedimus potestatem* are enclosed. The oaths are to be taken in open court, first by the four to whom the commission was addressed, and then to be administered by them to the other justices." Hamilton, *Quarter Sessions*. 2. For oaths of the justices of the peace, see Appendix, II and III, below.

The Qualifications of a Justice of the Peace. The justices of the peace were chosen from that rising and powerful middle class of landed gentry who superseded the feudal baronage, were disciplined in self-government in the county and parliament, and finally under the Stuarts asserted their power as the dominating political factor in the nation. The introduction of a bureaucratic element was prevented by the final disappearance of any fixed compensation. It is evident that the execution of the long list of statutes placed in their hands required more than ordinary ability and energy, and from time to time acts were passed to provide for the appointment of justices of capacity and high standing. The aim of the law was to consolidate the local authority in the hands of a single class, and as late as Elizabeth's reign it was necessary to exclude retainers and servants from the commission. Under Henry VI. a property qualification of £20 per annum was imposed upon all justices of the peace, and in case any county did not have in residence " sufficient persons, having lands and tenements aforesaid, learned in the law and of good governance," the Chancellor could put in discreet persons learned in the law even if they did not possess the required income.[1] Owing to the depreciation of money under the Tudors this qualification really amounted to nothing. Indeed it was scarcely necessary, for Lambard says that in practice the proportionate amount of property was taken into consideration when appointments were made.[2] In short, as the old statute ran, the justices of the peace were to be made of " the most sufficient knights, esquires, and gentlemen of the law of the said counties." [3]

Some knowledge of Latin was necessary, for the docu-

[1] 18 Henry VI., c. 11.

[2] *Eirenarcha,* 30.

[3] 13 Ric. II., s. 1, c. 8.

ments, writs, and records, relating to the office were for the most part written in that language, though English had begun to supersede it early in the Tudor period. Moreover a certain legal knowledge was absolutely essential to a proper discharge of the various functions. Lambard insisted that, while any discreet person could follow the various particular directions, a learning in the laws was indispensable when it came to examining witnesses, taking the oaths of jurors, and hearing and determining "according to the straight rule and course of the law." [1]

It need not be thought that the justices were uniformly active, efficient, and capable administrators. The gentry of the time were often extremely ignorant and brutal, although as a rule they were not far behind the general enlightenment of the age. At all events, the character of the justices was seriously called into question in a debate in parliament under Elizabeth. Mr. Glascock declared: "A justice of the peace is a living creature that for half a dozen chickens will dispense with a whole dozen of penal statutes . . . . If a warrant come from the Lord of the Council to levy 100 men, he will levy 200; and what with chopping in and crossing out, he will gain £100 by the bargain. Nay, if he be to send out a warrant upon a man's request to have any fetched in on suspicion of felony or the like, he will write the warrant himself and you must put two shillings in his pocket as his clerk's fee (when God knows he keeps but two or three hinds) for his better maintenance." [2] Another speaker seemed inclined to somewhat the same view, but Sir Francis Hastings declared that he had never heard justices of the peace taxed so in his life, and that for aught he knew they were men of quality, honesty, and ex-

[1] *Eirenarcha*, 46, 47.

[2] *Parliamentary History*, i, 944.

perience.[1] A proposal to censure Mr. Glascock was lost, especially after he explained that he did not intend to include all justices in his sweeping indictment. Apparently corruption in office is not limited to any age or country, and no doubt Lambard's characterisation of a justice of the peace is more ideal than real: "Thus then, our Parliaments, (intending to make the justice of peace an able judge) do require, that he come furnished with three of the principal ornaments of a Judge: that is to say with Justice, Wisdom, and Fortitude, for to that sum the words Good, Learned, and Valiant do fully amount. And under the word good, it is meant also that he loveth and fear God aright without the which he cannot be good at all."[2]

The Quorum. Along with the great local land-owners were those "skilled in the law," who exercised no little power in the transaction of business of any importance. The clause in the commission which gave two or more justices of the peace authority to hear and determine had a proviso that one of the specified justices should be present, (*quorum aliquem vestrum* A. B., C. D. &c., *unum esse volumus.*) The justices named in this proviso were the members of the commission who had a legal knowledge, and thus arose the technical expression "of the *Quorum.*" When an act was made conferring certain powers upon a specified number of justices, "one of them to be of the *Quorum,*" it meant that such powers could not be exercised unless there was present one of the persons skilled in the law mentioned in the proviso of the commission.

Number of Justices of the Peace. The number of justices assigned varied at different times and for different counties. The old law that six justices of the peace should be as-

[1] *Parliamentary History,* i, 945.

[2] Lambard, *Eirenarcha,* 30-31 (1602).

signed in every commission became obsolete and there seems to have been no limit to the number that a county could have.[1] In 1533 there were thirty justices in Devonshire[2] and in 1592, the number had increased to fifty-four.[3] Devon may be taken as a typical county. In writing of the large number of justices in each county Lambard says: "And (truly) it seemeth to me, that (together with the like ambitious desire bearing rule in some) the growing number of Statute laws committed from time to time to the charge of the justices of the peace, hath been the cause that they are now again increased to overflowing of each shire at this day."[4]

The Territorial District of the Justices of the Peace. In general the authority of the justice extended throughout the county in which he was commissioned and was limited to it. There were, however, certain important exceptions to this rule. "Some of the high nobilitie and chief magistrates for honour's sake" were placed in the commissions of a large number or all of the shires.[5] In Yorkshire and Lincolnshire there were separate commissions for the ridings and districts.[6] If the charter of a corporation had an exclusion clause, the county justices had no jurisdiction within its limits; but unless the provision *ita quod justiciarii comitatus se non intromittant* was inserted they were not enjoined from exercising their authority within its borders even if it had justices of its own.[7] The justice as such had no authority outside the borders of the county in which he was appointed,[8] and he could not summon a person out of his

[1] 12 Ric. II., c. 10.

[2] *State Papers*, v, 700.

[3] Hamilton, *Quarter Sessions*, 329.

[4] *Eirenarcha*, 32, 1602 ed.

[5] Smith, *Commonwealth*, ed. 1635, 158.

[6] Gneist, *Communalverfassung*, i, 551.

[7] Hale, *Pleas of the Crown*, ii, 47; Case de Abbe de St. Albans.

[8] Hale, ii, 50.

regular jurisdiction.[1] The extent of the authority of a justice over an offender who had fled into his district from another county was a question with Hale, although he thought the justice could examine, commit, and bind over the offenders and informers.[2] It was held in the reign of Edward IV. that if a justice pursued an offender into another county, he could not take him to the original county, but must imprison him where he was caught.[3]

The Borough Justices. The constitution of the office of justice of the peace in the boroughs must be sought in the numerous charters, grants, and orders, of which a few examples may be given here to illustrate the general principles followed. For a long time, many boroughs had enjoyed the privilege of excluding certain royal officers from their precincts, and the natural result was a powerful tendency toward decentralisation. To counteract this movement the practice of establishing borough justices was adopted in the fifteenth century. The effect, as may well be imagined, was highly favorable to the enforcement of general legislation within the boroughs.[4] Among the first charters organising borough justices was that granted to Nottingham in 1413. It provided that the mayor, recorder, and four burgesses should occupy that office.[5] The general practice of establishing municipal magistrates by char-

[1] Plowden, *Commentaries,* 37*a,* Platt's Case, 13 Ed. IV., f. 8.

[2] Hale, ii, 51.

[3] Plowden, 37, ed. 1761.

[4] Bateson, *Records of the Borough of Leicester,* II, pp. xxxiii and xxxiv. "In the fifteenth century the boroughs, as it were, with one accord turned actively to the work of setting by-laws on record; of proclaiming also through their by-laws what new statutes were being passed in Parliament, or what new royal proclamations and ordinances were being issued to the justices which especially concerned their town."

[5] Merewether and Stephens, *History of Boroughs,* 823.

ter may be said to have begun with Henry VI.[1] In 1440, Hull was made a county; the Yorkshire magistrates were excluded, and the mayor and thirteen aldermen elected by the burgesses were to be justices of the peace with full powers.[2] The subsequent charters followed the principle of stating specifically who were to be justices of the peace and excluding the county magistrates, although there were some exceptions. For example, in 1448, a Canterbury charter provided that the mayor and his successors were to be justices of the peace, that the county magistrates should not exercise any jurisdiction within the city, and that the mayor and commonalty should not be summoned to appear before the justices of assize or of the peace on the outside.[3] By the charter of the borough of Leicester granted by Edward IV. in 1464, the mayor, recorder, (learned in the law,) and four burgesses chosen by the close body of *Four-and-Twenty* were constituted justices of the peace of the borough with full powers. No guardian of the peace, justice, or commissioner assigned in the

[1] Merewether and Stephens, *History of Boroughs,* 795.

[2] *Ibid.,* 866-867.

[3] In the absence of a better authority, the following notices are taken from Merewether and Stephens. The Nottingham Charter of 1449 made the mayor, recorder, and four other good and lawful men justices of the peace, and the *non-intromittant* clause was added (p. 889). This was followed by another making the mayor and aldermen elected by the burgesses justices of the peace (p. 891). The London charter of 1462 provided that the mayor, recorder, and aldermen who had been mayors should be justices (p. 951). The Bristol charter of 1499 made the mayor and aldermen justices, and the *non-intromittant* clause was added (p. 1045). Oxford City and University charter of 1523 made the chancellor, vice-chancellor, and his deputy, justices of the peace for the town of Oxford and four surrounding hundreds. *Non-intromittant* clause was added (p. 1121). For Grantham, see p. 1035; Southwold, p. 1055; Litchfield, p. 1155; Newcastle, p. 789. The £20 qualification of Henry VI. did not apply to the boroughs.

county could interfere with any matters concerning the borough or compel the mayor, burgesses, or constables to appear before them.[1]

The crown was careful to maintain the privileges thus granted to boroughs. The statute of Henry VIII. centralising in royal hands the power of appointing justices of the peace expressly provided that the cities, boroughs, and corporate towns should enjoy their ancient franchises.[2] In Mary's reign complaint was made that the commissions granted in the shires had been used to supersede and clear those previously granted to cities and towns not counties of themselves. Therefore it was enacted that the power of such municipal justices should remain intact notwithstanding the fact that commissions were subsequently granted in the shires.[3]

Rights of the Justice of the Peace. No attempt was ever made to provide a regular salary for the justice of the peace; the attainment of economic and political power and the gratification of personal ambition were doubtless sufficient compensation. The property qualification apparently did not prevent the appointment of men of small substance as there were complaints in parliament of the extortions practised by impecunious justices. There were however certain perquisites attached to the office. An old law of Richard II. provided that the justices should hold their sessions three days together and receive four shillings a day each.[4] The Apprentice and Labour law of Elizabeth also enacted that the justices while sitting in the execution of the act should have five shillings a day.[5] The allowances were to

[1] Bateson, *Leicester Records,* ii, 280 and 365. In practice, ex-mayors were chosen as justices. *Ibid.,* xlviii.

[2] 27 Henry VIII., c. 24, s. v.

[3] 2 and 3 Philip and Mary, c. 18.

[4] 12 Ric. II., c. 10.

[5] 5 Eliz., c. 4, s. xxxi.

be paid out of the fines. The justice also had certain minor perquisites such as a portion of "Egyptian" goods which he seized,[1] and six pence of the twelve received when a recognizance of an ale-house keeper was taken.[2] The total yearly amount received from lawful sources, however, amounted to very little. Lambard thought it was wise to bestow the whole amount received for the work at the sessions "upon the defraying of their common diet." [3]

As a rule English law accords no special protection to officers like that given in continental practice. It appears however that an insult to a justice in open sessions was an actionable cause to be determined in the higher courts.[4]

Administrative and Judicial Control of the Justices of the Peace. In any well-developed legal system, the law which establishes an office and determines its functions must also provide for an administrative control on behalf of the state and remedies for individuals whose private rights are violated.[5] In English practice, no special institutions were ever constituted for administrative control or to provide remedies against officers as such.

In the sixteenth century, the central government exercised a disciplinary and supervisory control which was practically unlimited, but ordinarily the correction of the justices of the peace was left to the regular courts of law. The central control was exercised indirectly by the issue of writs and orders and directly by compelling the offenders to appear at the centre to answer for negligence and misdemeanors. Minor offences were heard in the regular courts. As a part of their ordinary business the justices of oyer and terminer by their commission were empowered

[1] 22 Henry VIII., c. 10.

[2] 5 Edward VI., c. 25.

[3] *Eirenarcha*, 585.

[4] Moore, *Reports*, 409, no. 554.

[5] Goodnow, *Administrative Law*, ii, 135.

to hear and determine negligence, transgressions, and other misdemeanors of justices. Cases of maladministration could be heard in the Star Chamber, Chancery, or Privy Council.[1]

The forms and processes by which control and remedies were secured were by no means fully worked out into a rigid system during the Tudor period. In the sixteenth century, much was undetermined in practice and legal theory. The crown, council, and central branches of judicature and administration were not limited by formal rules of procedure. Their constant aim was to secure the ends of state, and the methods employed were only an incident to their purposes. The entire nation seems to have generally submitted to the irregular methods of the government, for a protest was raised only against the irresponsible action of single members of the administration in imprisoning and determining arbitrarily.

The same irregularity seems to have prevailed in the expedients adopted to provide for appeals against the action of the justices of the peace. Appeal from court to court was unknown to the common law.[2] Local courts were always jealous of interference.[3] The evils of this independence were fully demonstrated in the fifteenth century, and Henry VII. in carrying out his policy sought to

[1] Moore, *Reports,* 656, no. 899; *Select Cases in Chancery,* no. 79; 4 Henry VII., c. 12.

[2] Pollock and Maitland, ii, 664.

[3] For example, in 1412, it was ordained by the mayor and community of Leicester "That if any one resident henceforth prosecute any writ before the chancellor of the lord king concerning threats, or a precept before the justices of the peace of the lord king against any one dwelling in the said town, by which writs or precepts any one shall lose any goods to the lord king or his ministers, he shall forfeit his gild in the mayor's grace." Bateson, ii, 225.

provide a remedy by legislation. In the fourth year of his reign, a statute was passed providing that anyone who was "hurted or greved" in anything by a justice of the peace should appeal to a justice or justices of the peace residing near. Failing to get a remedy there, the complainant was then to turn to the justices of assize, and if sessions were not to be held soon or the justices refused to right the wrong, he was then to show his grief to the king or his chancellor, who would examine the charge and on finding a justice of the peace in default eject him from the commission.[1] With a vagueness characteristic of much of the early legislation, this act says nothing of the actual procedure by which the remedy was to be secured.

The law also says nothing about making the quarter sessions a court of general appeal, and doubtless such was not the intention, although there is no evident reason why appeal should be allowed to other justices of the peace and not to the sessions. The old rule that the quarter sessions could hear appeals only in cases expressly provided by statute doubtless has its historical justification.[2] Indeed the appellate jurisdiction of the court of quarter sessions is a comparatively late development.[3] It was established during the century which saw abolition of the Star Chamber and the unlimited system of central control. Even then it was only special and statutory. It was acquired as a part of that larger and more dominating political power which the landed gentry secured over the crown. The documents of the sixteenth century clearly indicate that the government

[1] 4 Henry VII., c. 12. [2] Gneist, *Constitutional History*, 654.

[3] Gneist, *Self-Government, Communalverfassung und Verwaltungsgerichte*, 384. A slight beginning was made in the sixteenth century. For example, any person who had a grievance against the poor rate, or any acts of the local justices, could appeal to Quarter Sessions. 39 and 40 Eliz., c. 3, s. vi.

was more concerned with getting offenders punished than with providing a system of appeal to the quarter sessions.

However, the process of removing indictments and cases from the justices of the peace to the higher courts was fully developed. The writ of *certiorari* ordering the transfer of a cause to a higher authority was issued from Chancery upon "the sollicitation and by the meanes of some parties grieved, to the end that they may either traverse it above or there avoid it for insufficiencie of forme or matter." [1] The *certiorari* might command the justices to send up the record itself or the *tenorem recordi,* and if they failed to obey, "first an *Alias,* then a *Pluries* (*vel causam notis significes*) and lastly an attachment" went out against them.[2] Moreover, the *certiorari* was of force "to remove not only Endictments or other executory Records, wherein the justices of the peace can go no further, ... but also the Records of causes fully and lawfully heard and determined by them: to the end that they may be reversed and annulled in the King's Bench if good matter and cause do require it." [3] A cause removed from the justices of the peace could be transferred by a *mittimus* to any other court. The clause in the commission which provided that in difficult cases the justices of the peace should not proceed alone, in a way furnished a method by which individuals could in certain cases bring their cause before the assize justices.

The next great source from which a remedy was to be sought was the central government, that is, the Privy Council, Star Chamber, or Chancery. All discussion as to the

[1] Lambard, 485. The use of the *certiorari* to remove causes from the justices of the peace was recognised as early as the forty-first year of Edward III. *Le Livre des Assises.* London, 1679, p. 225. Pl. 22.

[2] *Ibid.,* 486.

[3] Lambard, 556.

STAND

England: In Its Origin and
earch & Source Works

3473, UNITED STATES

from the
store!

78

r # 2740905 Payment Da

AmazonMarketplaceUS# *112-982

112-9821490-0456213

FORN-0318-BB-2201

Quantity: **1**

The Office of Justice of th

Development (Burt F

Series, No. 24.)

ISBN: *158477102X*

AMZ ORDERS APTP, 800 AVONDALE AVE, , CC

158477102X

Th

M

MidtownScholar
BOOKSTORE

precise limits of these various branches is more or less unprofitable. Restricted perhaps in theory to special statutory matters or to causes not cognisable in ordinary courts, the Council and Star Chamber, which were one and the same body under Elizabeth, were not limited as to jurisdiction or process. They had and exercised arbitrary powers. An examination of the great number of petitions and complaints which are recorded in the documents reveals very meagre evidences as to appeals against the actions of the justices of the peace. The reason is not far to find. The people who came before the justices as offenders were in general representatives of the lower orders of society, who had neither the money, the influence, nor the ability to bring their causes to the notice of the crown. The power of the justices of the peace over property was comparatively limited, and the cases which came up to the central authority related for the most part to questions of possession.

A few examples will serve to illustrate the system of appeal to the centre. In the fourteenth century one Skelton, of the city of York, complained to the chancellor that several persons had attacked him and ousted him from his tenements, and that owing to the fact that the offenders were members of the same gild as the justices of the peace, the remedy should be provided by Chancery.[1] In the same century one Fraunceys complained that his rights in certain lands in Gloucestershire had been infringed, and he asked for an order from Chancery to the justices of the peace and sheriff of the county to see that he was restored to his own.[2] In another instance, an offender, whose goods the justices of the peace had ordered to be confiscated, appealed to Rome and got a citation of the officers who executed the order to appear there to answer for their action.

[1] *Select Cases in Chancery*, Selden Society, no. 79. [2] *Ibid.*, no. 70.

The officers then sought the determination of the matter in Chancery.[1] In 1578, one Thomas Chatterton complained to the Privy Council that in a forthcoming trial over possession, he was likely to be overborne and accused of felony. The Wiltshire justices of the peace and assize were promptly ordered to make an impartial trial.[2] When a county justice was accused of misdemeaning himself in taking examinations, the solicitor-general investigated the charge.[3] Another justice was put out of commission for wrongfully refusing to take a surety of the peace offered in due course.[4] In another case, one William Watkins of Brenocke, complained to the Privy Council that he and others had been detained in prison for six weeks for a crime of which they were innocent. Their trial being appointed for the assizes in that county, they sought a change of venue, alleging that the late sheriff was "alyed to the moste part of the justices of the peace and gentlemen of that county, whereby they stood in doubt of indyfferent tryall." The council ordered the justices of assize to look into the matter and take such a course as justice and equity required.[5] When one Nicholas Mullins complained that the county magistrates had left unredressed certain wrongs done him by two parties, the Council appointed two local residents to remedy the law's delay. Doubtless this latter practice was quite common, and for minor cases constituted the regular method of dealing with appeals for redress.[6]

The Custos Rotulorum. The Keeper of the Rolls was assigned by the last clause of the commission. He was al-

[1] *Select Cases in Chancery,* Selden Society, no. 121.

[2] *A. P. C.,* 1577-1578, 308. [3] *Ibid.,* 1586-1587, 385.

[4] Palgrave, *Authority of the King's Council,* 143.

[5] *A. P. C.,* 1589-1590, 319-320.

[6] Prothero, *Documents,* Duties of a Secretary, 167.

ways a justice of the peace and a member of the *Quorum*, and as such occupied a prominent position.[1] He had to attend the sessions in person or by agent, and his function was primarily to guard the records pertaining to the general sessions and to produce the writs, processes, precepts, and indictments as required by law at the sessions.

The Clerk of the Peace. This functionary was appointed by the *Custos Rotulorum* and held his position during the tenure of that official. He could discharge his duties in person or appoint an agent. His business was to enroll the proceedings of the sessions, read the indictments, draw the processes, record the proclamations of servants' wages, register licenses of laders and badgers of corn, and to certify transcripts of indictments, outlawries, attainders, and convictions before the justices of the peace to the King's Bench —in short, to keep a record of the doings of the justices in sessions and to attend to the general clerical work. The documents pertained to complaints, presentments, informations, indictments, processes, trials, judgments, executions, administrative acts of the sessions, regulation of wages of servants and artisans, recognisances of the peace and good abearing, and bailments.[2]

[1] Lambard, 371.

[2] *Ibid.*, 372.

CHAPTER VII

Process in Sessions of the Justices of the Peace

It is the purpose of this chapter to show the composition and working of a session of the justices of the peace at the close of Elizabeth's reign.[1] The method of transacting business did not materially change during the Tudor period. The machinery of the court was virtually complete before the accession of Henry VII., and the progress noted above was only the constant increase in the jurisdiction of the justices as individuals and in sessions.

The sessions of the justices of the peace were of three kinds: (a) discretionary, an assembly of two or more justices (one of the *Quorum*) at a certain day and place appointed, to enquire by jury or otherwise to take knowledge, and thereupon to hear and determine according to their power causes referred to their charge by the statutes and commission; (b) general or quarter sessions as required by law; and (c) special or petty sessions.

Discretionary Sessions. At such times as it was deemed necessary to hold what may be called here a discretionary session to distinguish it from the others, a writ was issued by any two of the justices of the peace, one of the *Quorum,* to the sheriff of the county commanding him to summon before them on a certain day and at a certain place twenty-four honest and lawful men from each hundred and twenty-

[1] Lambard, *Eirenarcha,* ed. 1602, is taken as the basis of this chapter.

four knights and other lawful men *de corpore comitatus.*[1] Each juror summoned was to have a property qualification of forty shillings per year. The sheriff was also commanded by the writ to instruct the coroners, stewards, constables, sub-constables, and bailiffs to be present at the coming sessions. He was to proclaim throughout the county the date and place of holding the sessions, and to appear himself with the names of the jurors who had been summoned, the coroners, stewards, constables, sub-constables, and bailiffs and the writ itself. The composition of the sessions was therefore as follows: two or more justices of the peace, the *Custos Rotulorum* or his agent, the clerk of the peace, the sheriff, coroners, bailiffs of franchises, constables of hundreds, stewards, the lawful and honest men summoned as jurors, those bound to keep the peace who were not specially required to appear at quarter sessions or gaol delivery, and all other citizens who chose to attend of their own accord. By the writ to the sheriff it is evident that twenty-four "law-worthy" men were to be returned from each hundred and twenty-four from the shire at large.[2] From these men the jury of inquest was sworn in. It was the practice in Kent to make up the general jury from the constables for the most part, and the particular juries from the representatives of the hundreds, the former to enquire of general matters and the latter of local affairs.[3] However, if a jury from a hundred made a presentment of an of-

[1] For copy of this writ, see Appendix, No. IV.

[2] The writ runs: "Venire facias coram nobis vel sociis nostris Justiciariis pacis . . . . tam 24 probos et legales homines de quolibet hundredo in balliva tua, quam 24 milites et alios probos et legales homines de corpore comitatus tui. . . . ."

[3] Lambard, 381. The burden of the work apparently lay upon the general jury, the others falling into disuse by reason of their cumbersome nature.

fence done in another part of the county, it was good in law.[1] Lambard says the jury of inquest ought to contain twelve men at least and that eighteen would not be amiss, though it was the common practice in Kent to have seventeen, nineteen, or twenty-one.[2]

On account of the great number of statutes the justices in making their charge rehearsed only the principal offences into which the jury was to enquire, although Fitzherbert held that the justices were bound to give to the jury "a charge of all such articles and things whereof they have authority and ought to enquire." Thus organised and charged with the execution of their duties according to the statutes, the jurors proceeded with their inquest, and returned indictments against offenders found guilty. These indictments were in the form of declarations and generally contained five articles: (a) name, surname, and place of the party indicted; (b) year, date, and place in which the offence was committed; (c) name of the party to whom the offence was done; (d) name and value of the thing in which the offence was committed; (e) manner and nature of the offence. Of course indictments which did not fall within their jurisdiction the justices could not receive; but they could deal with all presentments for causes mentioned in their commission and the statutes especially conferring powers upon them, and also those taken by the sheriff in the leet if that court had been legally held. There were, however, other sources of indictments or presentments than those given above. There were certain offences of which individual justices could take cognisance and return presentments to the sessions. Voluntary informations from private persons either by word or writing could be received,[3] but according to Lambard they were of force only

[1] Lambard, 282. [2] *Ibid.*, 383. [3] *Eirenarcha*, 481 *et seq.*

to stir up justices to recommend the matters to inquest. However, in some cases justices could receive information by witnesses as if indictment had been made by a regular jury.

Information, indictments, and presentments being taken, the next step was the procedure to be made upon them. There were, however, certain offences which lay without the final jurisdiction of the justices of the peace, and indictments of a certain character could be removed from the sessions at the solicitation of the party aggrieved. The indictments upon which the justices had no authority to determine were sent to the proper courts. The procedure in cases which clearly came within the powers of the justices varied according to circumstances. If the accused was present in court, and confessed to the indictment it was not necessary to issue a warrant for his apprehension, but he could be committed to prison until he paid his fine or gave security for it.[1] The indictments and presentments were merely accusations against the parties, and were made the bases for summoning the accused to trial, in case they were not already at the sessions. The process of issuing writs and causing the accused to appear differed also according to the circumstances.

A person so indicted upon his appearance in sessions could confess, if guilty, or stand trial. The trial could be carried out by the examination of the accused, the witnesses, and charges of the justices in certain cases without a jury, or, if the nature of the case demanded it, before a jury of twelve lawful men. The accused could challenge any of the jurors returned, upon certain technical grounds of incapacity to serve for lack of proper qualifications.[2] The trial then proceeded in the manner of an ordinary

[1] *Eirenarcha*, 490.

[2] *Ibid.*, 522.

jury trial in the king's court. If the accused was found guilty, judgment was pronounced upon him according to the provisions of the statute or, where not exactly defined, according to the discretion of the justices of the peace. The justices could punish officials for neglecting to carry out the judgments rendered.

The Quarter Sessions. The quarter sessions were those ordered to be held regularly four times a year on certain days prescribed by the statutes. The dates for holding the sessions were changed a number of times. The statute of 3 Henry V., c. 4 was the one supposed to be observed during the Tudor reigns. This provided for the holding of quarter sessions in the first week after St. Michael, the Epiphany, the Clause of Easter and the Translation of St. Thomas, the Martyr.

The length of time for holding the sessions was fixed by 2 Richard II., c. 3, as three days, if necessity required it. This custom however fell into disuse, and Lambard complained that the sessions did not often last over three hours. The procedure of the quarter sessions and the organisation of the court did not differ from the "discretionary sessions." In fact the only difference between the two was that certain statutes required the investigation of offences and the conviction of the indicted to be made at quarter sessions. The business of the justices in quarter sessions was not limited, however, to those special instances.[1] Quarter and discre-

[1] Criminal work of the mid-summer sessions of the peace at the Castle of Exeter in the fortieth year of Queen Elizabeth. *To be hanged:* Richard Rundell, horse stealing; Margery Pedell, cutting a purse; William Rowe, picking pockets; William Weeks, no depositions; John Delbridge, house breaking; Englishe Sanders (a woman), receiving stolen goods from Delbridge; Trystram Crosse, picking pocket and house breaking; John Capron, sheep stealing. *To be branded and set free:* Richard Payne, stealing clothes; Stephen Juell, Andrew Pen-

tionary sessions were as a rule held for the entire county, although there was considerable variation in practice.[1]

Special or Petty Sessions. Special sessions could be held in a given locality at the discretion of any two justices, one of the *Quorum,* and a large range of offences inquired into with the aid of a jury from the hundred. Lambard was of the opinion that whenever the term "sessions" was used indifferently in a statute conferring powers on the justices of the peace, the petty session could enquire into offences against it and hear and determine if the authority to do so

rose, John Reed, John Collacott, sheep stealing; Andrew Jordan, stealing clothes. *Acquitted:* Nicholl Hooper, stealing or receiving a shirt; Andrew Bragge, house breaking; Joan Cooke, stealing or receiving clothes; Nicholas Shilston, sheep stealing; Alice Wilkins, stealing a bed; Alice Bowden, receiving ditto; Richard Greenslade, stealing corn. *To be flogged:* Henry Sellock, no depositions; Temperance Drake, stealing clothes; Joan Bowne, no depositions; Phineas Horsham, sheep stealing; John Dodridge, no depositions; Thomasina Baron and Elizabeth Baron, stealing or receiving clothes; Alice Bagewell, stealing smock; William Ackland, stealing cheese, &c.; Blanche Symons and Thomas Jellard, stealing gloves, stockings, &c.; George Talman, sheep stealing; John Chalmers, sheep stealing. Hamilton, *Quarter Sessions,* 39.

[1] Lambard, 558-559. "For the manner is (in some shires) to summon yearely sixe standing Sessions of the Peace; in others 8; in others 12 or 16, and in others otherwise. All which is done chiefly upon pretence to ease the inhabitants of the Countie, for whom it would otherwise bee verie painefull to travell so often and so farre from all the partes of the Shire to any one place of the same. And, therefore, such as do maintain 6 or 8 sessions, do use to summon all the whole Shire to a couple of them, and to the residue they call onely such parts of the Shire as they doe specially appoint: but yet so that (upon the reckoning) each corner of the countrey giveth attendance at foure severall Sessions; which falleth out accordingly in those Shires where they have 12 or 16 sessions. For albeit that they do not at any one time summon the Shire to any one place (as the others doe), yet dividing their Shire into three or foure partes, and keeping foure severall sessions in each of those partes, they also (as well as the other) do serve their whole Country with foure sundry sittinges."

was given.[1] The chief work of the petty sessions was the examination of the offences of artificers, servants, laborers, vagabonds, rogues, sturdy beggars, and paupers and the punishment of petty thieves and other minor law breakers.

[1] Lambard, 580. For the execution of some statutes, three, four, or six justices were required to be present in the sessions.

CHAPTER VIII

Decay of Ancient Communal Institutions

Before the Tudor epoch, the justices of the peace as local police magistrates had made serious inroads upon the jurisdiction of the courts leet and sheriffs' turns.[1] During the sixteenth century, the justices took over a large portion of the work which had been left to the cumbersome communal courts. They were ever ready to do business and could exercise summary jurisdiction over numerous minor offences either as individuals or in petty sessions, while the local courts met only twice a year and required the presence of a large number of the members of the community.[2] Moreover several statutes transferred the jurisdiction of the old courts over minor offences to the justices.

The burden of police control was placed upon the justices and the local officers under them, although hue and cry was retained and the whole community could be called upon in case of need. As his title implies, the justice was primarily a police officer. His first care, therefore, was to prevent breaches of the peace by taking the surety of possible offenders either on his own motion or on a writ of *supplicavit* from the Chancery or at the request of some private party.[3] The procedure in such cases was simple: the justice issued a writ to the sheriff, constable, or other officer ordering him to appear with the person from whom the surety was de-

[1] See above. [2] Gneist, *Communalverfassung*, i, 308.

[3] For the writs, see Appendix, Nos. XVI and XVII.

manded, and in default of surety, the prisoner was committed to gaol.[1] If the recognisance was taken on writ of *supplicavit,* the justice had to send the document to the court from which the order proceeded. If, however, it was taken by the justice *ex officio,* he had to send or take it to the next session and deliver it to the *Custos Rotulorum* so that the recognisor could be summoned to appear and give an account of himself. The justice could also take surety for good abearing binding a party to demean himself well and to abstain from offences against law and order.

After an offence was committed, the justice could arrest the offender and conduct the preliminary examination, but only in very minor matters could he hear and determine. In conducting the preliminary inquest and making presentments to the higher courts which had authority to hear and determine, he relieved the community of a burden which had been extremely irksome in the middle ages. The capture by hue and cry and presentment by the representatives of the vills and hundreds became obsolete.[2] The justices assumed the work of examining persons arrested for manslaughter or felony. They took information as to facts and circumstances, and bound witnesses and offenders over to the next sessions of gaol delivery where the case was to be heard and determined. The single justice, however, had no authority to let such offenders out on bail; that could be done only by two justices at least, one of the *Quorum.* The justice could of course take the preliminary steps in cases which could be heard and determined in general sessions of the peace.

This development marks the transition to modern practice

[1] If an officer was standing near, the word of the justice was sufficient authority to make the arrest. Moore, *Reports,* 408.

[2] Gneist, *Communalverfassung,* i, 305.

in which police functions are given over to special officers and the community relieved of the burden of responsibility except for jury service and personal assistance in times of special need. While on the continent this inquisitorial work was given over to an official class, in England, it was placed in the hands of local residents co-operating with the representatives of communities.

APPENDIX OF ILLUSTRATIVE DOCUMENTS

No. I.

A Commission of the Peace. (*After 1590.*)

Elizabeth, Dei gratia Angliae, Franciae et Hyberniae Regina, fidei defensor, &c. Praedilecto et fideli Johanni Cantuar., archiepiscopo, &c., necnon praedilecto Thomae Egerton, militi, Domino custodi magni sigilli nostri, &c., salutem.

Sciatis, quod assignavimus vos conjunctim et divisim et quemlibet vestrum Justiciarios nostros, ad pacem nostram in comitatu nostro Kanciae conservandam: Ac ad omnia Ordinationes et Statuta pro bono pacis nostrae, ac pro conservatione ejusdem et pro quieto regimine et gubernatione populi nostri edita in omnibus et singulis suis articulis, in dicto comitatu nostro (tam infra libertates quam extra) juxta vim formam et effectum eorundem, custodiendum et custodiri faciendum. Et ad omnes contra formam ordinationum, vel statutorum illorum, aut eorum alicujus in comitatu praedicto delinquentes, castigandum et puniendum, prout secundum formam Ordinationum et Statutorum illorum fuerit faciendum: et ad omnes illos, qui alicui, vel aliquibus de populo nostro de corporibus suis, vel de incendio domorum suarum minas fecerint, ad sufficientem securitatem de pace, vel bono gestu suo, erga nos et populum nostrum inveniendam coram vobis, seu aliquo vestrum venire faciendum: et (si hujusmodi securitatem invenire recusaverint) tunc eos in prisonis nostris (quousque hujusmodi securitatem invenerint) salvo custodiri faciendum.

Assignavimus etiam vos et quoslibet duos, vel plures vestrum (Quorum aliquem vestrum A, B, C, E, F, &c., unum esse volumus) Justiciarios nostros, ad inquirendum per sacramentum proborum et legalium hominum de comitatu praedicto (per quos rei veritas melius sciri poterit) de omnibus, et omnimodis feloniis, veneficiis, incantationibus, sortilegiis, arte magica, transgressionibus, forstallariis, regratariis, ingrossariis, et extorcionibus quibuscunque: Ac de omnibus et singulis aliis malefactis et offensis (de quibus Justiciarii pacis nostrae legittime inquirere possunt, aut debent) per quoscunque, et qualitercunque, in comitatu praedicto factis, sive perpetratis, vel quae imposterum ibidem fieri, vel attemptari contigerit: Ac etiam de omnibus illis qui in comitatu praedicto in conventiculis contra pacem nostram in perturbationem populi nostri, seu vi armata ierunt, vel equitaverunt, seu imposterum ire, vel equitare praesumpserint: Ac etiam de omnibus hiis, qui ibidem ad gentem nostram mayhemandam, vel interficiendam de insidiis jacuerunt, vel imposterum jacere praesumpserint: Ac etiam de hostellariis, et aliis omnibus et singulis personis, qui in abusu ponderum vel mensurarum, sive in venditione victualium contra formam Ordinationum vel Statutorum, vel eorum alicujus, inde pro communi utilitate regni nostri Angliae, et populi nostri ejusdem editorum, deliquerunt, vel attemptaverunt, seu imposterum delinquere, vel attemptare praesumpserint, in comitatu praedicto: Ac etiam de quibuscunque vicecomitibus, ballivis, seneschallis, constabulariis, custodibus gaolarum, et aliis officiariis, qui in executione officiorum suorum (circa praemissa, seu eorum aliqua) indebite se habuerunt, aut imposterum indebite se habere praesumpserint, aut tepidi, remissi, vel negligentes fuerunt, aut imposterum fore contigerit, in comitatu praedicto: Et de omnibus et singulis articulis et circumstantiis et aliis rebus quibuscunque, per quoscunque et qualitercunque in comitatu praedicto factis sive perpetratis, vel quae imposterum ibidem fieri, vel attemptari contigerit, qualitercunque praemissorum, vel eorum alicujus, concernentibus plenius veritatem.

Et ad indictamenta quaecunque sic coram vobis seu aliquibus vestrum capta, sive capienda, aut coram aliis nuper Justiciariis pacis in comitatu praedicto facta sive capta (et nondum terminata) inspiciendum, ac ad processus inde versus omnes et singulos sic indictatos, vel quos coram vobis imposterum indictari contigerit (quousque capiantur, reddant se, vel utlagentur) faciendum et continuandum.

Et ad omnia et singula felonias, veneficia, incantationes, sortilegia, artes magicas, transgressiones, forstallarias, regratarias, ingrossarias, extortiones, conventicula, indictamenta praedicta caeteraque, omnia et singula praemissa, secundum leges et statuta regni nostri Angliae (prout in hujusmodi casu fieri consuevit, aut debuit) audiendum et terminandum: Et ad eosdem delinquentes, et quemlibet eorum, pro delictis suis per fines, redemptiones, amerciamenta, forisfacturas, ac alio modo (prout secundum legem et consuetudinem regni nostri Angliae aut formam Ordinationum vel Statutorum praedictorum, fieri consuevit, aut debuit) castigandum et puniendum.

Proviso semper, quod si casus difficultatis super determinatione aliquorum praemissorum coram vobis, vel aliquibus duobus, vel pluribus vestrum evenire contigerit: Tunc ad Judicium inde reddendum (nisi in praesentia unius Justiciariorum nostrorum de uno vel de altero banco, aut unius Justiciariorum nostrorum ad assissas in comitatu praedicto capiendas assignatorum) coram vobis vel aliquibus duobus, vel pluribus vestrum, minime procedatur.

Et ideo vobis, et cuilibet vestrum mandamus quod circa custodiam pacis, ordinationum, statutorum, et omnium et singulorum ceterorum praemissorum, diligenter intendatis: Et ad certos dies et loca, quae vos, vel aliqui hujusmodi duo, vel plures vestrum (ut praedictum est) ad hoc provideritis super praemissis faciatis inquisitiones, et praemissa omnia et singula audiatis et terminetis, ac ea faciatis et expleatis in forma praedicta facturi inde quod ad justitiam pertinet secundum legem, et consuetudinem regni nostri Angliae: Salvis nobis amerciamentis, et aliis ad nos inde spectantibus.

Mandamus enim tenore praesentium vicecomiti nostro Kanciae, quod ad certos dies et loca (quae vos, vel aliqui hujusmodi duo, vel plures vestrum ut praedictum est ei ut praedictum est scire feceritis) venire faciat coram vobis, vel hujusmodi duobus, vel pluribus vestrum (ut dictum est) tot et tales probos et legales homines de balliva sua (tam infra libertates quam extra) per quos rei veritas in praemissis melius sciri poterit et inquiri.

Assignavimus denique te praefatum Edw. Hoby, militem, Custodem Rotulorum pacis nostrae in dicto comitatu nostro; ac propterea tu ad dies et loca praedicta, brevia, precepta, processus, et indictamenta praedicta, coram te, et dictis sociis tuis, venire facias, ut ea inspiciantur, et debito fine terminentur, sicut praedictum est. In cujus rei testimonium, &c. Datum, &c.[1]

No. II.

Form of the Oath of a Justice of the Peace.

Ye shall swear that as justice of the peace in the county of Kent, in all articles in the Queen's commission to you directed, ye shall do equal right to the poor and to the rich after your cunning, wit, and power, and after the laws and customs of the realm, and statutes thereof made: And ye shall not be of counsel of any quarrel hanging afore you: and that ye hold your sessions after the form of statutes thereof made: And the issues, fines, and amercements that shall happen to be made, and all forfeitures which shall fall before you, ye shall cause to be entered without any concealment (or embezzling) and truly send them to the Queen's Exchequer. Ye shall not let for gift, or other cause, but well and truly you shall do your office of justice of the peace in that behalf: and that you take nothing for your office of justice of the peace to be done, but of the Queen, and fees accustomed, and costs limited by the statute: and ye shall not direct, nor cause to be directed, any warrant (by you to be made) to the parties, but ye shall direct them to the bailiffs of the said county, or other the Queen's officers (or ministers) or other indifferent persons, to do execution thereof: So help you God, and by the contents of this book.[2]

[1] From Lambard, *Eirenarcha*, ed. 1602, pp. 33-38.

[2] From Lambard, pp. 50-51.

No. III.

The Oath of Supremacy Required by 1 Eliz. c. 1 of all Ecclesiastical Officers and "Every Temporal Judge, Justice, Mayor and other Lay and Temporal Officer and Minister and every other Person" Receiving Wages or Fees from the Crown.

I, A. B., do utterly testify and declare in my conscience, that the Queen's Highness is the only supreme governor of this realm and of all other Her Highness' dominions and countries, as well in all spiritual or ecclesiastical things or causes as temporal, and that no foreign prince, person, prelate, state or potentate hath or ought to have any jurisdiction, power, superiority, pre-eminence or authority, ecclesiastical or spiritual, within this realm; and therefore I do utterly renounce and forsake all foreign jurisdictions, powers, superiorities and authorities, and do promise that from henceforth I shall bear faith and true allegiance to the Queen's Highness, her heirs and lawful successors, and to my power shall assist and defend all jurisdictions, pre-eminences, privileges and authorities granted or belonging to the Queen's Highness, her heirs and successors, or united or annexed to the imperial crown of this realm: So help me God and the contents of this book.

No. IV.

Writ to a Sheriff to Summon a Session of the Peace.

Edwardus Hoby, miles, et Radulphus Hayman, armiger, duo Justiciar. dom. reg. ad pacem in comitatu Kanciae conservandam nec non ad diversas felonias, transgressiones, et alia malefacta in dicto comitatu perpetrata, audiendum et terminandum, assignatorum, vicecomiti ejusdem comitatus, salutem.

Ex parte dictae dominae Reginae tibi praecipimus, quod non amittas propter aliquam libertatem in balliva tua, quin eam ingrediaris, et venire facias coram nobis, vel sociis nostris

Justiciariis pacis, &c (tali die &c.) proxime futuro apud Maidstone in comitatu praedicto tam 24 probos et legales homines de quolibet hundredo in balliva tua, quam 24 milites et alios probos, et legales homines de corpore comitatus tui (tam infra libertates quam extra) quorum quilibet habeat 40 sol. redditus terrarum et tenementorum libere per annum ad minus: ad inquirendum tunc et ibidem super hiis quae ex parte dictae dominae reginae eis injungentur.

Scire facias etiam omnibus Coronatoribus comitatus tui, Seneschallis, Constabulariis, Sub-constabulariis, et Ballivis libertatum, infra hundreda et libertates praedicta, quod sint tunc ibi ad faciendum et perimplendum ea quae ratione officiorum suorum sunt facienda.

Proclamari praeterea facias per totam ballivam tuam, in locis idoneis praedictam Sessionem pacis ad diem et locum praedict. fore tenendam.

Et tu ipse tunc sis ibidem, ad faciendum, et exercendum ea quae ad officium tuum pertinent: et habeas ibi tunc, tam nomina Juratorum, Coronatorum, Seneschallorum, Constabulariorum, Sub-constabulariorum, et Ballivorum praedict. quam hoc praeceptum.

Datum sub sigillis nostris apud Shoreland in comitatu praedicto, 16 die Martii, anno regni dictae dom. nostrae Reg. Eliz., Dei gratia, &c., 44.[1]

No. V.

Testimonial of a Sturdie Beggar, who had been punished under 39 Eliz. c. 4.

John at Stile, a sturdie vagrant beggar, of lowe personage, red-hayred, and having the naile of his right thomb cloven, was the sixt day of April in the fortie and one yeare of the Raigne of our soveraigne Ladie Queene Elizabeth, openly whipped at Dale in the said countie for a wandring Rogue, according to the lawe: and is assigned to passe forthwith

[1] From Lambard, p. 366.

from parish to parish by the officers thereof, the next straight way, to Sale in the countie of Middlesex, where (as hee confesseth) hee was borne (or dwelled last by one whole yeare &c. if the case be such) and he is limited to be at Sale aforesaid, within tenne daies now next ensuing, at his perill.[1]

No. VI.

Record of a Complaint against Forcible Entry, and the Investigation made by a Justice of the Peace, and Certified to the Queen's Bench.

Memorandum quod octavo die mensis Januarii, anno Regni Dominae nostrae Elizabethae, &c. Quaestus est mihi Samsono Lennard, uni Justiciariorum dictae Dominae Reginae, ad pacem in dicto comitatu conservandam assignatorum, quidam A. B. de Wrotham in dicto comitatu, Yeoman, quod C. D. de Wrotham praedicta, et nonnulla alii pacis dictae Dominae Reginae perturbatores ignoti, in domum mansionalem ipsius A. B. in Wrotham praedicta, manu forti ingressi sunt, et ipsum A. B. inde disseisiverunt, ac eandem manu forti et armata potentia adhuc tenent: ac proinde petiit a me sibi in hac parte remedium apponi. Qua quidem querimonia et petitione audita, ego praefatus S. L. immediate ad dictam domum mansionalem personaliter accessi ac in eadem domo adtunc inveni praefatum C. D. et quosdam E. F. et G. H. &c. domum illam vi et armis, manu forti et armata potentia, viz: arcubus et sagittis, gladiis, pugionibus galeis et loricis tenentes contra formam statuti in Parliamento Dom. Richard nuper Regis Angliae secundi, anno regni sui decimo quinto tento, provisi: ac contra formam diversorum aliorum statutorum. Ac propterea ego praefatus S. L. praedictos C. D., E. F. et G. H. adtunc et ibidem arrestavi, proximaeque gaolae dictae Dominae Reginae apud Maidstone in dicto comitatu duci feci, ut de dicta manu forti tentione per visum et recordum meum convictos ibidem moraturos quousque fines dictae Dominae Reginae pro

[1] From Lambard, p. 190.

transgressionibus suis praedictis fecerint. Datum apud Wrotham praedictam sub sigillo meo die et anno supradictis.[1]

—

No. VII.

Form of "Mittimus" to Gaoler Sent with Persons Arrested for Forcible Entry.

George Chowne, one of the justices of the peace of our Soveraigne Ladie the Queen's Majestie, within her said countie of Kent, to the keeper of her Majestie's gaole at Maidstone, in the said county, and to his deputie and deputies there and every of them, greeting. Whereas upon complaint made unto me this present day by A. B., of Wrotham, in said countie, Yeoman, I went immediately to the dwelling house of the said A. B. in Wrotham aforesaid, and there found C. D., E. F. and G. H., of Wrotham aforesaid, Labourers, forcibly, and with strong hand, and armed power, holding the said house, against the peace of our said Soveraigne Ladie, and against the forme of the statute of Parliament thereof made in the 15 years of the raigne of the late K. Richard the second. Therefore I send you (by the bringers hereof) the bodies of the said C. D., E. F. and G. H., convicted of the said forcible holding, and by mine owne viewe, testimonie and recorde: commanding you in her Majestie's name to receive them into your said gaole, and there safely to keepe them, until such time as they shall make their fines to our said Soveraigne Ladie for their said trespasses, and shall be thence delivered by the order of the law of the land. Hereof faile you not, upon the perill that may follow thereof. Yeoven at Wrotham aforesaid, under my seale the day and yere abovesaid.[2]

[1] From Lambard, *Eirenarcha,* 140.

[2] From Lambard, p. 141.

No. VIII.

Record of a Riot Drawn up by Justices of the Peace and Sheriff or Under-sheriff.

Memorandum quod xx die Januarii, anno regni dominae nostrae Elizabethae, Dei gratia &c. Nos Henricus Brooke miles, Dominus Cobham, Dominus Guardianus Quinque Portuum et Ed. Hoby miles, duo Justiciariorum dictae dominae Reginae ad pacem in comitatu praedicto, &c. assignatorum, et Martinus Barnham adtunc vicecomes ejusdem comitatus, ad gravem quaerimoniam et humilem petitionem A. B. de C. in dicto comitatu Yeoman, in propriis personis nostris accessimus ad domum mansionalem ipsius A. B. in C. praedicta, ac tunc et ibidem invenimus D. E. F. G. H. I. de C. praedicta, Laborers, ac alios malefactores et pacis dictae dominae Reginae perturbatores ignotos, ad numerum decem personarum modo guerrino arraiatos, viz: gladiis, pugionibus galeis, loricis, arcubus et sagittis, illicite et riotose aggregatos, et eandem domum obsidentes, et multa mala in ipsum A. B. cominantes, in magnam pacis dictae Dom. Reg. perturbationem, ac populi sui terrorem et contra formam statuti in parliamento Domini Henrici nuper Regis Angliae quarto, anno regni sui decimo tertio tento editi et provisi. Ac propterea nos praefati Dominus Cobham et Edw. Hoby et Martinus Barnham, praedict. D. E. F. G. H. I. &c. tunc et ibidem arrestari ac proximae gaolae dict. Dom. Reg. in comitatu praedicto duci fecimus, per visum et recordum nostrum de illicita congregatione et riota praedict. convictos, ibidem moraturos quousque finem dict. Dom. Reg. proinde fecerint. In cujus rei testimonium huic praesenti recordo nostro sigilla nostra apposimus. Datum &c.[1]

No. IX.

Presentment of an Unlawful Assembly.

Juratores pro Domina Regina praesentant, quod primo die mensis Octobris, anno regni dominae nostrae Elizabethae, Dei

[1] From Lambard, pp. 316-317.

gratia &c., tricesimo A. B., C. D., E. F. &c. apud quendam locum infra parochiam de O. in comitatu praedicto, Anglice vocatum le Old Court, inter horas decimam et undecimam ante meridiem ejusdem diei, vi et armis, tam invasivis, quam defensivis, videlicet, gladiis, pugionibus, baculis, arcubus, sagittis, tunicis ferreis et tormentis, seipsos congregaverunt et assemblaverunt: ac tunc ibidem intenderunt, conati sunt, et practicaverunt, vi et armis, illegitime, et ex authoritate sua propria, secare, et prorsus evertere, prosternere ac destruere quoddam caput unius aquae ductus, Anglice vocatum *a conduit head*, tunc ibidem in fundo cujusdam R. S. de O. praedicta in comitatu praedicto generosi, existens et cursum aquae in ipso habens, ea intentione, ut idem caput aquae ductus praedict. ex tunc apertum et vacuum remaneret ac jaceret: Et ulterius, quod super querimonia inde facta coram T. W. uno Justiciariorum pacis dictae dominae reginae in comitatu praedicto, omnes et singuli praedicti A. B., C. D., E. F. &c. tunc et ibidem per eundem Justiciarium requisiti sunt ac jussi (per proclamationem in nomine dictae dominae Reginae tunc ibidem per eum palam factam) ad habitationes, loca et domos suas, unde venerant, se inde in pacifico modo retrahere, retirare, discedere et reverti: quae quidem proclamatio tunc ibidem modo et forma sequentibus habita et facta est, viz: praedictus T. W. Justiciarius tunc ibidem fecit alta voce unam *Oyes* ac tunc ibidem immediate haec verba Anglicana sequentia palam alta voce pronunciavit, dicens scilicet: The Queene oure Soveraigne Lady chargeth and commandeth all persons (being assembled) immediately to disperse themselves and peaceably to depart to their habitations, or to their lawful businesse upon the paines contained in the acte lately made against unlawful and rebellious assemblies: And God save the Queene. Et ulterius, Juratores praedicti dicunt, quod non obstante dicta proclamatione modo et forma praedictis per praefatum Justiciarium tunc ibidem facta et habita, iidem tamen omnes et singuli praedicti A. B., C. D., E. F., &c. in dicto loco vocato le Old Court infra parochiam de O. praedicta in dicto comitatu per spacium duarum horarum, immeditate et continue post dictam proclamationem, sic ut praefertur factam et habitam, sequentium, seditiose et felonice insimul remanserunt et continuaverunt, in magnum dict. dom. Reg. contemptum, ac contra pacem, coronam et dignitatem suas, necnon contra formam diversorum statutorum in hujusmodi casu provisorum et editorum.[1]

No. X.

Presentment Concerning a Broken Bridge.

Juratores pro Dom. Reg. presentant, quod pons publicus et communis, situs in alta regia via super flumen de Medway, infra parochiam de A. in comitatu praedicto (vulgariter dictus Aileseford Bridge) est et per aliquot annos jam proxime lapsos fuit valde ruinosus, et in maximo decasu ob defectum reparationis, adeo ut subditi dictae dominae Reginae, in, super, trans, vel ultra dictum pontem, per se, vel cum eorum equis, bigis aut cariagiis, ire, redire, aut transire, sine magno vitae discrimine non audent aut possunt, ad commune nocumentum omnium vicinorum, et compatriatarum in dicto comitatu habitantium, quorum interest ratione negotiorum suorum illac transire: Et ulterius quod prorsus nescitur, quae personae, quaeve terre, tenementa, aut corpora corporata, et politica, eundem pontem, aut aliquam inde parcellam, ex jure, aut ex antiqua consuetudine, reficere et reparare debent, aut consueverunt.[2]

No. XI.

Form of Indictment for Failure to Work upon the Highways.

Juratores pro domina regina presentant, quod ubi die Martis in septimana Paschae jam ultimo praeteritur, scilicet septimo die mensis Aprilis, anno regni dominae nostrae Elizabethae, Dei gratia, &c., tricesimo, A. B. tunc constabularius villae de C. in dicto comitatu et D. E. et F. G. tum guardiani

[1] From Lambard, Precedents, in *Eirenarcha.*

[2] From Lambard, *Eirenarcha,* Precedents.

ecclesiae parochialis de C. praedicta in comitatu praedicto existentes, vocatis ad se multis aliis parochianis dictae parochiae de C., tunc et ibidem elegerunt quosdam I. S. et R. N. duas honestas ejusdem parochiae personas, in supervisores pro uno anno integro tunc proxime sequenti, pro emendatione et reparatione altarum regiarum viarum infra dictam parochiam de C. ducentium a villis mercatoriis, ad villas mercatorias: ac etiam tunc ibidem nominaverunt et appunctuaverunt sex dies, viz: 1, 2, 3, 4, 5, 6 dies mensis Maii tunc proxime sequentis, pro dicta emendatione dictarum viarum et nominatim pro emendatione illius viae regiae ibidem quae est inter &c., atque de eisdem sex diebus (sic per eos ut praefertur nominatis, et appunctuatis) dederunt palam postea, scilicet die dominico dictae Paschae tunc proxime sequenti, publicam notitiam in dicta ecclesia parochiali: quidam tamen T. W. tum et adhuc parochianus de C. praedicta in comitatu praedicto existens, ac tum habens et occupans in dicta parochia de C. in comitatu praedicto unam integram carucatam terrae arabilis (Anglice dictam Ploughland) nullum dictis primo, secundo, et quarto diebus dicti mensis Maii anno supradicto prorsus invenit, aut misit currum instructum (Anglice dictum a waine or cart furnished) equis, bobus, aut aliis animalibus et necessariis, secundum morem patriae ibidem: nec ullos habiles homines, erga emendationem et reparationem dictarum viarum aut earum aliquam, sive aliquam inde parcellam: sed inde tunc ibidem voluntarie fecit defaltam: in dictae dominae reginae contemptum, ac contra formam diversorum statutorum in hujusmodi casu provisorum et editorum.[1]

—

No. XII.

Indictment for Extolling the Authority of the Pope.

Juratores praesentant pro Domina Regina, quod I. S. de C. in comitatu praedicto, Clericus, xx die mensis Aprilis anno regni serenissimae dominae nostrae Elizab. Dei gratia etc.,

[1] From Lambard, *ibid.*, Precedents.

tricesimo, apud D. in comitatu praedicto, scienter, considerate, malitiose, et directe palam in praesentia multorum dict. dominae reginae nostrae nunc subditorum, affirmavit et defendit authoritatem papae Romani ecclesiasticam in hoc regno Angliae, prae antea usurpatam, hiis expressis verbis Anglicanis sequentibus, viz: I swere by the blessed masse, and will avow that our holy father the pope of Rome, is the supreme head of the church of England, in magnam derogationem regiae authoritatis, et praerogativae dictae dominae Reginae nostrae, ac contra coronam et dignitatem suam, necnon contra formam diversorum statutorum in hujusmodi casu editorum et provisorum. Et quod A. B. de D. predicta in comitatu praedicto, *Waxchandlor,* sciens ipsum I. S. dicta verba loquutum esse, ac dictam dicti papae authoritatem modo et forma ut praefertur, defendisse, ipsum I. S. apud D. praedictum, postea, scilicet 22 die dicti mensis Aprilis anno supradicto, consolatus est et comfortavit, ex industria et ex proposito, et ad eam intentionem ut idem A. B. promoveret, et efferret praefatam dicti papae authoritatem usurpatam, in perniciosissimum aliorum exemplum, ac contra coronam et dignitatem dictae dominae Reginae nostrae nunc, ac etiam contra formam diversorum statutorum in ejusmodi casu provisorum et editorum.[1]

No. XIII.

Indictment for Keeping a Tippling House without License.

Juratores pro domina Regina praesentant, quod A. B. de C. in dicto comitatu Yeoman, vicesimo die mensis Octobris, anno regni dictae dominae nostrae Eliza. Dei gratia &c., tricesimo, et continue multis diebus postea, videlicet, usque 1 diem dicti Octobris, anno supradicto apud C. praedict. in comitatu praedicto, obstinate, atque ex autoritate propria ipsius A. B., et sine ulla Justiciariorum pacis dictae dominae reginae in comitatu praedicto admissione aut allocatione, assumpsit super se custodire, et custodivit unam communem Tabernam (Anglice

[1] From Lambard, *ibid.,* Precedents.

vocatum a common Tippling house) et ibidem dicto vicesimo die et dictis diebus tum postea, communiter et publice vendidit cervisiam, panem et potum, Anglice dictum Beere, diversis dictae dom. reg. ligeis et subditis. In dictae dominae reginae contemptum, ac contra formam cujusdam statuti in parliamento domini Edwardi nuper regis Angliae sexti, tento apud Westmon., anno regni dict. domini Edwardi quinto in hujusmodi casu provisi et editi.[1]

—

No. XIV.

Indictment of a "Vagabond and His Releever."

Juratores pro domina regina praesentant, quod A. B. nuper de C. in dicto comitatu *Scavelman,* aetatis septem annorum et amplius, ac corpore sano, valente, potente, atque ad laborandum habili existens, nullam autem habens terram, aut ullum magistrum, nec aliqua utens licita merchandiza, arte, vel mysterio unde sibi victum parare posset, x die Decembris anno regni dom. nostrae Eliza. Dei gratia &c., 41 apud E. infra hundredum de W. in comitatu praedicto, et multis aliis in locis dicti comitatus, hac illac passim vagatus est mendicans, ac per W. P. de E. praedicta in dicto comitatu Yeoman, constabularium dicti hundredi de W. (in quo sita est villa de E. Praedicta) postea, viz: undecimo die dicti mensis Januarii anno supradicto apud E. praedict. in comitatu praedicto inventus est vagarans, et mendicans, ac per eundem constabularium tunc ibidem deprehensus est inordinate se gerens, tanquam vagabundus, et mendicus validus: contra pacem dictae dominae reginae, ac contra formam diversorum statutorum in diversis parliamentis dictae dominae reginae nunc inde provisorum et editorum: Et ulterius, quod G. H. de E. praedicta in dicto comitatu Yeoman, sciens praefatum A. B. modo et forma praedictis vagantem et mendicantem, eundem tamen A. B. dicto decimo die anno supradicto in domo ipsius G. H. mansionali apud E. praedict. in comitatu praedicto hospitavit, et eidem A. B. tunc

[1] From Lambard, *ibid.*, Precedents.

ibidem panem et potum voluntarie dedit, in contemptum dictae dominae reginae, ac contra formam statutorum praedictorum.[1]

No. XV.

Indictment for Keeping and Playing Unlawful Games.

Juratores pro domina regina praesentant, quod A. B. de C. in dicto comitatu *Tipler,* secundo die Septembris, anno regni Dom. Reg. Eliz. Dei gratia &c., tricesimo, et continue post dictum diem anno supradicto usque primum diem mensis Octobris anno supradicto, apud C. praedictam in comitatu praedicto quendam communem locum jaciendi globos (vocatum Anglice *a common Bowling Alley*) pro lucro ipsius A. B. proprio, et ad ludendum tunc ibidem cum globis (Anglice vocatis Bowles) illicite tenuit, custodivit ac manutenuit, contra formam cujusdam statuti in parliamento dom. Hen. nuper regis Angliae, 8. tento anno regni sui 33, in hujusmodi casu provisi et editi: Et quod I. S. de C. predicta in dict. comitatu, *Labourer,* et tres aliae personae ignotae, dicto secundo die Septembris anno supradicto, dictum communem locum visitaverunt, ac tunc ibidem cum globis Anglice vocatis Bowles, insimul et illicite luserunt, contra formam statuti praedicti.[2]

No. XVI.

Writ for a Person Required to Give Surety for Keeping the Peace.

Elizabeth, by the grace of God &c. To our shiriffe of Kent, the constables of the hundred of Wroteham, the Borsholder of the towne of Ightham, and to all and singular our Bailifes and other our ministers in the saide countie, as well within the liberties as without, greeting. Forasmuch as A. B. of Wroteham aforesaid Yeoman, hath personally come before George Bing, of the said town Esquier, one of our justices of the peace within the said countie, and hath taken a corporal oth, that he

[1] From Lambard, *ibid.,* Precedents. [2] *Ibid.*

is afraid that one G. D. of Shipborne, in the saide countie Yeoman, will beate, wound, maime, or kill him, or burne his houses, and hath therewithall praied suretie of the peace against the said G. D. Therefore we command and charge you, joyntly and severally, that immediately upon the receipt hereof, you cause the said C. D. to come before the said G. B., or some other of our said justices, to finde sufficient suretie and mainprise, aswel for his appearance at the next Quarter Sessions of our peace to be holden at M. in the said county as also for our peace to be kept towards us and all our liege people, and chiefly towards the said A. B., that is to say, that he, the said G. D. shall not doe, nor by any meanes procure or cause to be done, any of the said evils, to any of our saide people, and especially to the saide A. B. And if hee, the saide G. D. shall refuse thus to doe, that then immediately without expecting any further Warrant, you him safely convey or cause to bee safely conveyed, to our next pryson in the said countie, there to remaine untill he shall willingly doe the same; So that hee may bee before our saide justices, at the sayde next Generall Sessions of the peace to bee holden at M. aforesaide, then and there to answere unto us for his contempt in this behalf. And see that you certifie your doing in the premisses to our saide justices at the saide Sessions, bringing then thither this precept with you. Witnesse the said G. B. at Wroteham aforesaid, the fourth day of August &c.[1]

—

No. XVII.

Form of Recognisance for Keeping the Peace.

Memorandum, quod quarto die Julii, anno regni dominae nostrae Elizab., Dei gratia, &c., 41, R. P. de F. in comitatu praedict. Yeoman, in propria persona sua venit coram me, I. Levison, milite, uno Justiciariorum dict. domin. Reginae ad pacem in dicto comitatu conservandam assignatorum, et assumpsit pro seipsos sub paena viginti libr. Et. H. I. de L. in

[1] From Lambard, *ibid.*, pp. 80-81.

comitatu praedicto Yeoman; Et I. F. de M. in eodem comitatu Husbandman, tunc et ibidem in propriis personis suis similiter venerunt, et manuceperunt pro praedict. R. P. (videlicet) quilibet eorum separatim sub paena 100 solid. quod idem R. P. personaliter comparebit coram Justiciariis dict. dom. Reginae ad pacem ad proximam generalem sessionem pacis in comitatu praedicto, ad faciendum et recipiendum quod ei per curiam tunc et ibidem injungetur: Et quod ipse interim pacem dictae domin. Reginae custodiet erga ipsam dominam Reginam, et cunctum populum suum et praecipue versus M. N. de Ightham praedict. Yeoman, Et quod dampnum vel malum aliquod corporale aut gravamen praefato M. N. (aut alicui de populo dict. Domin. Reginae quod in lesionem aut perturbationem pacis ipsius Domin. reginae cedere valeat) quovismodi non faciet, nec fieri procurabit. Quamquidem summam xx lib. praedict. R. P. et quilibet manucaptorum praedictorum praedictas seperales summas 100 solid. recognoverunt se debere dictae Domin. Reginae de terris et tenementis, bonis et catallis suis quorumlibet et cujuslibet eorum, ad opus dict. Domin. Reg. haeredum et successorum suorum fieri et levari, ad quorumcunque manus devenerint, si contigerit ipsum R. P. praemissa vel eorum aliquod in aliquo infringere, et inde legitimo modo convinci. In cujus rei testimonium &c.[1]

[1] From Lambard, *ibid.*, p. 99.

VITA.

THE writer of this dissertation was born in Indiana in 1874. He studied at De Pauw University, graduating in 1898 with the degree of Ph. B. and with membership in the Phi Beta Kappa Society. He studied at the University of Oxford, England, 1898-99. He was a student at Cornell University in the autumn of 1899, and was Professor Tyler's fellow-elect in American history. From 1900 to 1902 he lectured for the Educational Committees of Co-operative Societies in England and Wales on history and economics. In 1902 he entered the School of Political Science, Columbia University. He held the George William Curtis fellowship in Columbia, 1902-03, and was awarded the Toppan prize in Political Science and Constitutional Law in 1903. He received the degree of M. A. from Columbia in 1903, and continued his studies during 1903-04. He attended the lectures of Professors Burgess, Clark, Goodnow, J. B. Moore, Osgood, Robinson, and Seligman, and was a member of the seminars of Professors Burgess, Clark, Moore, Seligman, and Robinson.